THE CRAFT OF PUBLIC SPEAKING

Colin M. Barron

Other Books by
Colin M. Barron

Running Your Own Private
Residential or Nursing Home

THE CRAFT OF PUBLIC SPEAKING

Colin M. Barron

The Craft of Public Speaking by Colin M. Barron.

First edition published in Great Britain in 2016 by Extremis Publishing Ltd.,
Suite 218, Castle House, 1 Baker Street, Stirling, FK8 1AL, United Kingdom.
www.extremispublishing.com

Extremis Publishing is a Private Limited Company registered in Scotland
(SC509983) whose Registered Office is 51 Horsemarket, Kelso, Roxburghshire, TD5
7AA, United Kingdom.

A CIP catalogue record for this book is available from the British Library.

ISBN: 978-0-9934932-5-6

Typeset in Goudy Bookletter 1911, designed by The League of Moveable Type.
Printed and bound in Great Britain by IngramSpark, Chapter House, Pitfield, Kiln
Farm, Milton Keynes, MK11 3LW, United Kingdom.

Cover artwork and stock images are Copyright © Pixabay.
Cover design and book design is Copyright © Thomas A. Christie.
Author image is Copyright © Thomas A. Christie.
Some internal diagrams utilise elements of royalty-free imagery from OpenClipart.org.

Contents

Foreword

by Janet Thomson

This title of this book does exactly what it says on the tin – or, in this case, the cover. Public speaking is a **craft**, something that has to be honed and practised. Dr Colin Barron has the enviable skill of being able to take a subject and break it down into practical and understandable components that can be delivered effectively. He has developed this expertise throughout his working life in the medical (both NHS and holistic) environment, and has now applied the same methodology to the field of public speaking.

This book is a user-friendly guide to the world of public speaking, both as a lay person and in a professional capacity. It is as masterfully constructed as the many informative, entertaining talks and presentations that Colin has given over many years.

I can recall one instance when I could have made great use of some of the tips in this book. I had been asked to speak at a company dinner in front of 150 employees. The lady who booked me said that as chairperson she got to choose the speaker and the subject, and could I please speak about how to lose weight. My designated slot was 60 minutes. I had a folder of acetates for the overhead projector (before the advent of PowerPoint!) and arrived, as agreed, thirty minutes before I was due to speak, in order to set up. The venue was the back of a pub in a marquee.

I approached a man in a cloth cap (for those of you of a certain age think 'wheel-tappers and shunters') who said to me in a strong Derbyshire accent: 'Ello luv, are you the act?' To my astonishment he led me into a room of coalminers and engineers, with the only female present being the chairperson. Imagine their delight and anticipation at waiting to hear my talk! If I had had the 'General Montgomery Approach' (which you will learn about later), I would have been much better prepared. I survived because I had a few cartoon slides in the presentation that I spontaneously built a completely different presentation around. To this day I have no idea what I actually said, but the audience gave me a standing ovation and asked me to stay for a drink so I must have done something right!

If I'd had Colin's approach, I would not have had to 'fly by the seat of my pants' – something a professional speaker should never do. In fact, had I read this book years ago I would have picked up so many valuable tips. I have no doubt my trainings and talks would have been the better for it.

Whether you want to stand up at a local meeting and effectively get your point across without feeling intimidated, or you are a professional speaker looking to refine your skills, within these pages you will find informative, well-researched and entertaining practical guidelines and techniques that I am sure will prove to be invaluable.

I have been lucky enough to see Colin in action, and his combination of intellect and just the right amount of humour on any of his chosen subjects is both engaging and instructive. I wholeheartedly recommend this book, and encourage you to take the information within and build it into your own unique style. Be yourself, enjoy yourself, and remember to remember: before you can inspire anyone else, you must first inspire yourself.

Janet Thomson
www.powertochange.me.uk

5 May 2016

The Craft of
Public Speaking

Colin M. Barron

Chapter One

How this book came about

'Nothing in life is more important than the ability to communicate effectively.'
Gerald Ford

I have been interested in public speaking since my late teens. When I was at school I was a shy, timid child who shunned social situations and blushed easily. Then in early 1974, when I was in my sixth year at Greenock Academy and just 17 years old, I was asked to give a talk on a religion of my choice to the rest of the sixth year as part of our weekly Religious Education (RE) class.

It was the first time I had given a presentation to an audience and I even had the use of an overhead projector which, back then, was regarded as state-of-the-art technology. Much to my surprise the presentation went extremely well. I felt relaxed throughout and even put a bit of humour into my delivery.

I was stunned at my achievement because I expected that my social anxieties would have affected my performance. In reality they weren't an issue. Looking back at this incident 42 years later, with all the knowledge I now have about the workings of the human mind, I can understand how this happened. My social anxieties were triggered by certain situations, which did not include speaking in front of an audience. Almost certainly they originated from a specific incident (or a series of them) some years before which had been forgotten by my conscious mind.

Not only did I give my presentation without any anxiety, I found that I enjoyed doing it and I have remained that way ever since.

On the other hand, if my two perfectionist, over-critical parents (both doctors) had attended that presentation they would have criticised my performance, giving me a lifelong fear of public speaking (which many people have). My parents never heard me give a speech until 1990. As expected my mother had some criticisms of my approach (she was a member of the local Toastmistresses), but by then I had so many successful speeches and presentations under my belt that her remarks had no effect on my confidence as I knew she was just nit-picking.

In October 1974 I started the medical course (M.B. Ch.B.) at Glasgow University and soon made an interesting discovery. Most of the lectures were poor. Two notable exceptions were those given by Dr John Shaw-Dunn and Professor Joe Scothorne of the Anatomy Department, who both had excellent deliveries and employed humour to great effect.

As the medical course progressed the lectures got even worse. I made a personal resolution that if I ever had to give such talks then I would do the best I could to make them funny, concise and interesting. During the medical course there were a few opportunities to give presentations and I was also required to give lectures to the nurses when I became a Senior House Officer (SHO) and then a registrar in Ophthalmology.

However it was when I became a private nursing home owner in 1985 that I had to give presentations and speeches on a regular basis as Scottish chairman of the British Federation of Care Home Proprietors (BFCHP). It was then that I decided to read every book on public speaking that I could find. In my personal opinion the best of the lot was Dale Carnegie's classic tome *How to Develop Self Confidence and Influence People by Public Speaking* which was first published in 1926 and based on course material first used in 1916. Carnegie is of course best known for his later publication *How to Win Friends and Influence People*, which originally appeared in 1937 and has sold several million copies.

In January 1990 I attended a three-day course on public speaking and presentation skills at the Columbia Hotel in London, which was run by the late John May. This seminar was a revelation because, although I had some degree of natural ability as a public speaker, John taught me the importance of good technique, particularly in structuring a presentation.

At the time of writing I am almost 60 and have been listening to other people's speeches and presentations for 42 of these years. Most of these talks have been awful and the most common fault has been poor technique.

The problem as I see it is that most people do not receive any kind of tuition in public speaking. They have never been on a course on presentation, nor have they read any of the books that have been published on the subject. Instead they copy what they see other people doing and (without realising it) make a number of fundamental mistakes, which I will explain in detail later. In addition, the introduction of laptop computers has lead to the phenomenon of 'Death by PowerPoint' which I will also deal with later in this book.

One of the ironies of public speaking is that it doesn't matter how bad your lecture or speech is; the chairman of the meeting will always praise you, saying you made a wonderful presentation and the audience will applaud you though in reality they are just delighted that you have finally finished your monologue and they can go home.

In this book I hope to open your eyes to the common mistakes people make when presenting, and offer my suggested remedies. As Ralph Waldo Emerson once put it: 'All the great speakers were bad speakers at first'.

Chapter Two

Common faults in presentations and public speaking

'If you can't explain it simply,
you don't understand it well enough.'
Albert Einstein

In this chapter I will describe some of the most common errors in public speaking and their remedies. I would emphasise that many of these topics will be covered in far greater detail in subsequent chapters.

Speeches which are too long

As someone once put it, 'a speech may be immortal but it does not have to be eternal'. Or as Winston Churchill once said: 'A speech should be like a woman's skirt - short enough to attract attention but long enough to cover the important points'. In other words, a talk of any kind can be too lengthy but it can never be too concise since most people in the audience are dying for it to be over.

The traditional length of a university lecture is one hour, but the ideal maximum length for good recall of the information imparted is 25 minutes. You should always speak for less than the allotted time, e.g. if you are asked to speak for 20 minutes then speak for 15. I can assure you that no-one in the audience will complain! The way you keep to time is by rehearsing your presentation at least four times using a stopwatch.

Presentations which are too complicated
Many presentations fail because the lecturer attempts to put over too many points, or too complicated an argument, in one session. Instead you should aim to make a few simple points in an easily understandable way. When I was in my fourth year of medical school we used to get a weekly lecture on Pathological Biochemistry which was Pathologically Boring. It was a subject that was so complicated that it could not really be learned from a lecture, only from slow meticulous study from a textbook.

Misuse of visual aids
The advent of PowerPoint has meant that anyone with a computer can produce high-quality slides. Unfortunately this technology is often grossly misused, resulting in the phenomenon of 'Death by PowerPoint' which we have all experienced.

Lack of aims
Many presenters never really think about what the aim of their presentation should be. As the late Dale Carnegie once said: 'A talk is a voyage with a purpose and it must be charted. The man who starts out going nowhere, generally gets there'.

Lack of structure

In my personal opinion this is the most common fault of all. Most talks have no clear structure. A good presentation should have a clearly defined beginning, middle and end.

Lack of advance planning

Many presentations fail because the speaker hasn't checked out the venue beforehand. As I will explain later in this book, it is very helpful to find out everything possible about the chosen venue such as the layout of the room. A site visit (if at all possible) can be very helpful.

Poor delivery

Again this is a very common problem since most people don't know how to project their voice to the back of the room or to put feeling into their presentation. Speaking too fast and mumbling words are also bad faults.

Poor posture and body language

A good presenter should look and feel confident. Eye contact should be made with the members of the audience (and I will explain how to do this in a later chapter). Always stand facing your audience and never turn your back on them.

Misuse of humour

Jokes and humour can enliven a presentation but, as a rule, if you are not a funny person in everyday life you should not try to be a comic when you give a talk. Any jokes used should match the topic you are speaking about, and funny stories about things that have happened to you are often preferable to off-the-shelf jokes.

Chapter Three

Preparing for a speech or a presentation

'Dig your well before you're thirsty.'
Will Rogers

In August 1942 it looked as though Britain was about to lose the war in North Africa. General Rommel's seemingly unstoppable *Afrikakorps* had been halted at a defence line which ran through a little-known town with a small railway station, called El Alamein. Diplomats and top military men were so convinced that Cairo would fall that they had already started to burn top secret papers. After nearly eighteen months of defeats and military disasters, it seemed that it was game over for the British 8th Army.

Then something happened which changed everything. A new commander was put in charge of the British and Commonwealth forces. General Bernard Law Montgomery was a deeply flawed character who irritated his superiors and yet was really wonderful at motivating the men who served under him. He was also a very able commander.

Winston Churchill was so concerned about the situation that he flew to Egypt in an RAF Consolidated

B-24 Liberator bomber lacking proper seats, insulation, heating or pressurisation. Flying anywhere was a highly dangerous proposition in 1942. Churchill met Montgomery and implored him to attack Rommel immediately with the tanks and troops he had, but the general declined.

You see, Montgomery knew that if he waited till late October then he would have more troops, tanks, guns, vehicles, aircraft and supplies making the defeat of the *Afrikakorps* a certainty rather than just a possibility. Montgomery was proved right and the resulting battle of El Alamein in late October 1942 was the beginning of the end for the Axis forces in North Africa, paving the way for the total destruction of Nazism.

Montgomery held the view that he would never fight any battle unless he knew in advance that he would definitely win. He would set things up with an overwhelming superiority of numbers and firepower so that he could never lose. Incidentally the only time Monty departed from this strategy was before the ill-fated 'Operation Market Garden', involving the use of vulnerable airborne troops to capture key bridges in Holland in September 1944. If any of you have seen Sir Richard Attenborough's 1977 film *A Bridge Too Far* (or read any of the numerous books on the subject), you will know what a disaster that turned out to be.

However, Monty's usual method was to carry out a tremendous amount of advance planning and allocate huge resources to a battle so that failure was impossible. I have termed this the 'General Montgomery approach', and this is what I use in everyday life, whether it is for preparing a speech or presentation or organising a training course or seminar.

I used the 'General Montgomery Approach' when I sat my exam in clinical hypnotherapy with Stephen Brooks' organisation (then called the British Society of Clinical and Medical Ericksonian Hypnosis and now called British Hypnosis Research) in March 1999. At the start of the training a year earlier Stephen had given everyone a printed list of 100 questions, some of which would be asked by the examiner during the oral part of the exam.

I copied all the questions onto my computer and then, after careful study, wrote down my suggested answers. I discussed the more difficult questions with people who had completed the course and my tutors, constantly updating the answers to take account of this new knowledge. When I had got the responses as good as I thought they could possibly be, I printed out the completed document and carried a copy everywhere with me. Any time I had a few minutes to spare I would take out the document and read it until eventually everything was committed to memory. I now knew that I would get 100% in the oral part of the exam.

Next was the question of case histories. We had to submit three of them, so I had them done months in advance and then had my course tutors look at them so that I could amend them to take account of their feedback.

The last thing I did to ensure success in the exam was to persuade one of the course tutors to give myself and one of my fellow students (Molly-Ann Smith) a mock exam, an exact dress rehearsal of the real thing, which took a whole day, a month before our real exam. Feedback on our performance, both positive and negative, was noted by both of us.

On 19th March 1999 we both sat the exam. Johnny Lovell, a top hypnotherapist and NLP practitioner, was our examiner. Not only did we pass but we were both awarded distinctions, only given to people who had scored more than 95%. Incidentally, two other medical doctors sat the exam around this time and both passed, though they didn't get distinctions and I would attribute this to the fact that they didn't do as much advance planning and rehearsal as I did. In other words, they didn't use my favoured 'General Montgomery Approach'.

All this has relevance to the delivery of a speech, a lecture or even a whole training course. It is my personal experience that one reason why many people fail at public speaking and presentations is because they don't prepare properly. They simply turn up at the venue with a few notes scribbled on the back of an old envelope, wing it and expect everything to go well.

So how does the 'General Montgomery Approach' work when it comes to presentations and speeches?

The first principle is that you should find out exactly what is required of you at the event you are speaking at. Here are the questions you should be asking both yourself and the event organiser, if there is one:

- What is the purpose of my speech or presentation?
- What is the topic?
- What points do you want me to cover?
- How long should the presentation last?
- Are there facilities for PowerPoint such as a laptop and data projector (if you are using one)?
- Is a flip chart or whiteboard available (if you need one)?
- Will a lectern be provided?
- How many people will be in the room?
- What is the seating arrangement?
- Is there going to be a panel of speakers or will I be on stage alone?
- Does the room have air conditioning?
- Does the room have fans?
- Does the room have windows?
- Do the windows open?
- Will I be provided with a microphone and PA system?
- Is the microphone fixed on a lectern or stand or is it mobile, or are you using radio mikes attached to my clothing?
- Has time been allocated for questions at the end?
- How long will question time be?
- Who else will be speaking?

- Can I see a copy of the programme?
- Is the room noisy or quiet?

Many of these questions may seem pretty obvious, but you would be surprised how many speeches and presentations fail because these simple points haven't been checked out.

I would suggest you visit the venue where your presentation is to be delivered, to check out the layout of the room. Obviously this is not always possible, for example if you live in Aberdeen and you are expected to give a talk in Bournemouth, but some information on the layout of the room can often be obtained through phone calls, post, emails and the Internet. I would be the first to admit that I have been caught out many times because I didn't check out the venue.

I was once asked to give a presentation at a hotel in San Diego. When I actually got there I had my talk carefully scripted in advance, but soon found I had just about every factor conspiring against me. I was expected to give my talk at the end of a boozy lunch, so everyone was drowsy. I was in the centre of the room, so half the audience were behind me. There was no PA system and there was a very noisy glass-fronted cabinet fridge in the room which couldn't be turned off, so many people couldn't hear what I was saying. Furthermore, the management had difficulty finding an overhead projector and screen (this was in pre-PowerPoint days), adding to my anxiety. It was a disaster.

On another occasion in the mid-eighties I was asked to give a presentation on private nursing homes to the local Rotary Club at one of their monthly dinners at the Dreadnought Hotel in Callander. There were similar problems to those encountered in San Diego. My speech came at the end of a heavy meal with alcohol, so everyone felt drowsy and tired. I was in the middle of the room with my back to half the audience.

Worse still, my visual aid this time was 35mm photographic slides. The Rotary Club supplied a projector, carousel and operator but things went wrong. Unfortunately the operator loaded the carousel wrongly, so my carefully prepared slides were presented upside down in reverse order. The chairman's nose must have been longer than Pinocchio's when he concluded the evening by saying that I had given an excellent presentation!

You would be surprised how often there are problems with the room which are not foreseen.

Several years ago I was the organiser (and one of the speakers) at a conference at a hotel near Heathrow Airport. The windowless room seemed ideal as it incorporated air conditioning. On the day though, the noise from the aircon unit tended to drown out the speakers. Because it was a relatively small room with good acoustics I did not consider that a PA unit with microphones was required; something which I now realise was a mistake. We had to turn off the air conditioning so that people could hear the speakers. Even though it was only mid-March the room became warm and one audience member complained that she 'couldn't stand the heat', so we had to get a couple of electric fans into the room. This cooled everyone down but then some delegates complained that they couldn't hear the presenters because of the noise of the fans, so we turned them off only to discover that a group of saxophone players was practising in the next room. Oh well; at least the lunch was good!

It is also useful to obtain a copy of the programme to ensure you are given a decent slot. Conference organisers have a tendency to give you the worst possible slot, e.g. the last presentation of the morning (when everyone is wanting their lunch) or last thing in the afternoon (when everyone is dying for the thing to finish). The best possible one is first thing, after the conference chairperson has made their opening remarks.

So in conclusion, adequate preparation is one of the cornerstones to making a good presentation. As Abraham Lincoln once said: 'Give me six hours to chop down a tree and I will spend the first four sharpening the axe'.

Chapter Four

The importance of structure

'Good order is the foundation of all things.'
Edmund Burke

I have listened to hundreds of speeches and presentations over the last four decades. Most of them have been awful and the most common fault has been a lack of structure.

A good presentation or speech (even an impromptu one) should have a definite beginning, middle and end, and this should be signposted to the audience. As a lay preacher in the 19th century put it:

> 'First I tell them what I'm going to tell them, then I tell them what I tell them, then I tell them what I've told them.'

One of the oldest pieces of advice ever given on public speaking, it appears in Dale Carnegie's classic tome *How to Develop Self Confidence and Influence People by Public Speaking* which was first published in 1926. It was also a key part of John May's course on public speaking which I attended in January 1990. (I have been using this approach with some additions, as I shall explain shortly) ever since. The interesting thing is that, in the 26 years since I did the John May course, I have listened to hundreds of speeches and presentations given by other people and only on **one** occasion have I witnessed another presenter use this extremely powerful technique.

So how would you do this in practice? Well let us suppose you were asked to give a talk to the local Rotary Club about how you feel about plans to build 500 new homes in a local beauty spot near to where you live. You might say something like this:

> 'And in this presentation I am going to explain all the reasons why we should not have these new houses. I will be talking about the noise and pollution during construction, I shall be explaining how local roads won't be able to cope with the extra traffic, I shall be expounding on how our children could be put at risk of being knocked down and lastly I shall show that this town doesn't have the facilities, such as sewage capacity and car parking spaces, to cope with this vast number of new residents.

Then you would go through each of these points *in exactly the same order* as in your summary, fleshing each one out in considerable detail, and then you would end something like this:

'So that then is a look at the reasons why I oppose this new development. There will be noise and pollution during construction. Local roads won't be able to cope with the extra traffic. Our children could be at risk of being knocked down. And our town doesn't have the sewage capacity or car parking spaces to cope with these extra residents.'

You may ask why it is necessary to do this. The answer is that it *helps people to remember* the main points of your presentation. By signposting your talk in this way and summarising the main points at the end, it greatly helps people to understand and remember what you have just said.

It is a technique that has been used for decades in television, particularly in news programmes. For example, the BBC *Nine O'Clock News* starts with a very brief summary of the main news headlines. *News at Ten* on ITV used to do it even more dramatically with a 'bong' (courtesy of a chime from 'Big Ben' preceding each bullet point). News programmes usually conclude with a quick summary of the main headlines, while some take things even further by having a summary of what is still to come halfway through the broadcast.

So it is a universally accepted technique for helping people to remember and if you are not using it in your speeches and presentations then I suggest you start doing so. I have employed the method in every talk and lecture I have given since January 1990, often to great effect.

How recall varies with time
We remember the beginning and end of a presentation quite clearly but tend to forget information in-between, as the graph below indicates:

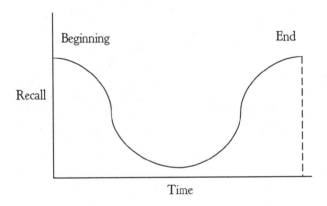

The longer a presentation goes on, the greater this 'dip' becomes, so it is inadvisable to speak for more than 25 minutes at a time. Ideally a lecture should be as short as possible: three very short talks with a break in-between is better than a single long one.

Of course, two things have to be added to this method to complete the plan of a presentation: what I call the 'Opening Hook' and a punchy ending, both of which I will explain in more detail shortly. So the plan for your speech or presentation should be as follows:

1.   Opening hook
2.   Summary of main points of presentation
3.   Delivery of each of these points in same order just described
4.   Summary of points just delivered
5.   Punchy ending

The Opening Hook
The opening hook serves the same function as the pre-credits action sequence in a James Bond movie. It is there to wake up the audience, get their attention, build rapport and get them in a receptive mood for what is to follow. There are many different forms of 'opening hook', as I shall explain:

The Dramatic Statement
- 'If a Jumbo jet with 500 passengers crashed every day in flames there would be public outcry. Yet that is the same number who die each year from heart disease.'
- 'Five million people unemployed by 2025. That is what may happen if we sign this treaty.'
- 'Ten years from now all petrol and diesel cars could be banned if this new legislation goes ahead.'

The Rhetorical Question
- 'Do you know what the largest employer in the UK is?'
- 'Do you know long a rocket would take to reach Venus?'

A combination of the Dramatic Statement and the Rhetorical Question
- 'How much water does it take to manufacture a ton of steel?
  In fact it takes a hundred gallons, the same amount the average family uses in a month.'

The Prop
Almost anything relevant to your presentation can be used. For example if you are giving a talk on the benefits of cycling you could carry a bike onto the stage, dump it down with a crash and then say something like this:

> 'That's one advantage of bicycles. You can take them anywhere. And in this presentation...'

Another easier way to gain the same effect without having to carry a bike would be to wear a cycle helmet as you go on stage and then plonk it down noisily. You could even go the whole hog and wear cycling clothing to give your presentation.

The Joke Hook

A good joke can serve as an opening hook. If possible the joke should be in some way connected with the topic of the presentation. Or you could use something which is very general. Here is one joke opening hook I have used a couple of times:

'The purpose of this conference is to explore the scientific research behind hypnosis. Interestingly, research has shown that once a talk goes on for more than 15 minutes, 97% of the audience are engaged in private sexual fantasy. I have timed my presentation and it lasts 18 minutes. So I think you should all thank me right now for all the pleasure I am going to give you.'

The Anniversary Hook

One way to open a presentation is to find out what happened on the same date many years before and then link it in some way to the topic of your speech. For example, if you were asked to speak on December 7th you might say something like this:

'Ladies and gentlemen. Today is December 7th. On this date in 1941, 353 Japanese aircraft sent numerous American warships to the bottom of Pearl Harbour.' [At this point you might show a colour slide from the film *Tora, Tora, Tora* on your PowerPoint, or even play with a model of a Japanese Zero fighter.]] '75 years later, our businesses are also in danger of being sunk by this new EU legislation.'

You can find out what happened on a certain date by consulting the book *A Dictionary of Dates* by Cyril Leslie Beeching (Oxford University Press, 1993), or many other similar tomes such as *The Book of Days* by Bob Monkhouse (Arrow Books, 1981). And of course, nowadays you can obtain this information on the Internet.

By the way, never open your speech by announcing that you are not good at public speaking. I have seen people do this a few times. At one conference I attended two nursing home owners opened their joint presentation by telling the audience that they weren't good public speakers. They were right: they weren't. But did they really have to signpost their deficiencies in this fashion?

Ending your presentation

The ending of a speech or presentation is crucial yet most people make a hash of it. As Henry Wadsworth Longfellow once said: 'Great is the art of beginning... but greater is the act of ending'. Do you know the worst possible way to end a talk? Then just say something like this:

- 'Oh well, that's all I've got to say so I will just stop there.'

- 'How much time have I got left?'
- 'Oh look at the time. I'd better stop.'

Now these are not endings. They are cop-outs.

So how should you end a talk? As already described, you should have already summarised the main points of your oration. Then, using non-verbal communication, you should signal to the audience that the presentation is about to end. You can do this by slowing down, and deepening, your voice.

It is a method that has been used in the cinema for decades. I am sure you have all seen a movie and known a moment or two before the words 'The End' appeared on the screen that the film was about to finish. Generally what happens is that one or two of the main characters make a profound comment and look into the distance, appropriate music is heard on the soundtrack, and the camera slowly zooms or tracks out so that we finish with a wide angle shot of the scene. It is part of the 'grammar' of film and TV productions that they often start with the camera zooming in on a building and end with a slow zoom out. If you want to see an example of what I mean then watch the ending of *633 Squadron*. Air Marshal Davies (played by Harry Andrews) makes the heartfelt comment 'You can't kill a squadron', the end title music by Ron Goodwin starts, and the camera slowly zooms and tracks backwards to end with a wide angle shot of RAF Bovingdon with the words 'The End' superimposed as the music reaches a climax.

A similar method should be used to end your presentation. You non-verbally signal that end is only a moment away and then finish with a punchy quote or a call to action. John May always recommended using the words 'and finally' at this point, since you are telling the audience that their ordeal is almost over. John once said that you should really start a talk with the words 'and finally', since they are the words delegates most want to hear because they are dying for your speech to be over! You can also end with a joke, though if possible this should relate to the topic of the talk. I will be talking more about the use and abuse of humour in a subsequent chapter.

Chapter Five

Writing your speech or presentation

*'One day I will find the right words
and they will be simple.'*
Jack Kerouac

There are really three possible ways in which a speech or presentation can be prepared. They are as follows:

No notes or script of any kind

Some speakers I know are of the opinion that this is the best way to do it, since the resulting speech or presentation appears 'spontaneous' and there is no danger of the speaker spending much of the time 'eyes down' looking at a prepared script instead of maintaining eye contact with the audience.

I can (and have) done it this way. The only caveat is that I would only use this method if I really knew my material and was speaking about a topic I was extremely familiar with. For example, when I gave presentations on Thought Field Therapy, Hypnotherapy and the Power of the Subconscious Mind to the local stroke club I didn't use any kind of script or notes since I already knew so much about the subject. I did though spend some time the night before, planning the lecture in my mind and blocking out a rough structure to my talk.

Furthermore, it is my experience that speakers who say they 'never use a script' are in fact using the same words, sentences, paragraphs and whole sections of material that they have used many times before. So in reality they **are** working from a script, it is just that it is a mental script and not a paper one.

Another disadvantage to this method is that the resulting presentation is often full of 'ums' and 'ers' etc., and the speaker may use too many words to express an idea or even repeat whole sections by mistake - something that can be avoided with a full script and several rehearsals.

A full written script

This is the exact opposite to the method given above in which every single word, pause, and slide is put down on paper. This is actually my preferred method, as I believe it has a number of advantages which are as follows:

a)   Accurate timing is easier. As a rule of thumb you should allow 100 words of text for every minute you have to speak, so for a 20 minute presentation you need to write 2000 words.

b)   It is easier to prepare the presentation in spoken English rather than written English. Spoken English and written English are polar opposites, and later in this chapter I will be explaining a bit more about this topic.

c)   It is easy to convert the script into handouts or to give a complete draft to journalists after you have spoken.

d)   There is little chance of fluffing your lines or forgetting a section.

e)   It is easy to repeat the presentation to a new audience a few months later since everything is written down.

Using bullet points written on index cards

This is really a 'halfway house' between the two methods described above. You write down the main bullet points on a series of cards which you hold in your hand and then improvise your dialogue as you go along. If you do use this technique, remember to number each card so they can be easily re-assembled in the correct order if you accidentally drop them. Just six cards which are not numbered can be arranged in 719 different combinations, all of which are wrong. It is not a technique I have ever used, but some people swear by it.

Written English vs spoken English

Many presentations fail because they are drafted in written English rather than spoken English. The two types of English are polar opposites. For example, in traditional written English one might write 'could not', 'would not', 'cannot' etc., whereas in spoken English 'couldn't', 'wouldn't' and 'can't' would be more effective. Another very important difference between the two types of English is the question of the repetition of a word in the same sentence or paragraph.

In traditional written English there is a concept called 'elegant variation' which states that it is grammatically poor to repeat the same word (or a similar sounding word) in a single paragraph. Compare these two examples:

> Watched by scientists, the rocket rose from its launcher. The rocket rose higher into the sky. Soon it was hard to see the rocket against the blue sky and bright sun.

After sub-editing this text in accordance with the principle of elegant variation, the revised paragraph would read like this:

> Watched by scientists the rocket rose from its launcher. The missile climbed higher into the atmosphere. Soon it was hard to see the projectile against the blue sky and bright sun.

What I did in this example was use three different words to describe the same object, i.e. 'rocket', 'missile' and 'projectile'. I also used 'atmosphere' to replace one of the two uses of the word 'sky'.

The interesting thing is that in spoken English, the opposite applies as the repetition of a word (or a series of words) close together in a piece of text can be very effective: a technique which is known as anaphora.

Probably the most famous use of anaphora is Winston Churchill's famous speech from 1940: 'We shall fight them on the beaches. We shall fight them on the landing grounds. We shall fight in the fields and the streets, etc.'. And of course in more recent times there has been Tony Blair's well known utterance about 'Education, education, education'.

So if you were writing an article, you might express one of the common ills of the NHS as follows: 'This country needs more hospital beds, extra GPs and an increase in the number of nurses'.

If you were giving the same information in a speech, it would be more effective to say something like this: 'This country needs more hospital beds... This country needs more GPs... And above all, this country needs more nurses'.

Speeches do not need to be absolutely correct grammatically. There is a belief among some public speakers that you should never use notes of any kind. In his book *How to Make Effective Business Presentations and Win*, John May has this to say about the topic: 'Presenters who habitually speak without notes are geniuses or misguided. The idea that we should not have notes comes from an old but now disregarded rule of the House of Commons that speeches may not be read. Today this is broken all the time by front-bench politicians'.

So how do you go about writing a complete speech for a presentation? Both Dale Carnegie (1926) and John May (1985) have suggested that you start off by obtaining a large envelope in which you accumulate scraps of paper, backs of envelopes etc., in which you have jotted down ideas which you might like to incorporate in your speech. These ideas may come to you at different times of the day, when you are engaged in other activities (e.g. shaving, bathing, walking the dog, cooking, putting on make-up, ironing etc.). It is important that you write down these ideas as soon as they appear in your conscious mind so that you don't lose them. This might be termed the 'incubatory' phase of speech writing.

After a week or two, when you feel you have accumulated sufficient ideas you can put these scraps of paper into your desired chronological order and start writing your speech.

To ensure that you write using spoken English I suggest that you read your presentation out loud while you are drafting it. This is where Voice Recognition Software (such as Dragon) can be very helpful, as you can simply speak your presentation out loud and the computer will transcribe it into words. (You will of course have to go through the resulting text to correct the many howlers which the VR software will make.)

Another tip in writing speeches is that you should use prose which conjures up pictures but also involves the other sensory systems; namely touch, smell, taste and hearing.

Compare these two examples of prose to see what I mean:

1)   'I walked across the courtyard on a sunny day.'

2)   'As I walked across the rough, sun-scorched terracotta tiles of the courtyard - so hot they nearly burned my feet - I felt the blazing sun beating down on my bare, exposed shoulders. I could still taste the Keo beer in my mouth as I smelled freshly-cut grass and the oily exhaust fumes of lawnmowers. The noise of the two-stroke engines nearly deafened me as the gardeners mowed the lawn.'

In the second example I have added more detail to involve all the senses which would result in audience members actually seeing the pictures I described, hearing the sounds I suggested, smelling odours and even experiencing tastes I had implied.

Analogies, metaphors and similes can be very powerful if used in the text of a speech. Metaphors in particular are very potent as the unconscious mind picks up the meaning behind them. That is the reason they are often used by hypnotherapists. One of the most famous metaphors ever used in a speech was Winston Churchill's famous 1946 comment that 'An Iron Curtain has descended across the continent'. This was all the more powerful because at the time many people went to theatres and music halls and were used to a heavy fireproof safety curtain descending at the end of a performance.

Tell stories to illustrate your point. In the early nineties I had to give a talk to a group of local authority people about the importance of gaining the cooperation of care home owners in improving standards. So I told the well-known story of the villagers in the Middle Ages who were trying to get a donkey to go into the back of a cart. They kicked it, they pulled it, they pushed it, they screamed abuse at it. Eventually they collapsed with exhaustion. They simply could not force the animal into the back of the wagon. Then a young boy stepped out from the crowd who had gathered to witness this spectacle. He took a carrot from his pocket, held it in front of the donkey and gently led it into the cart.

The moral of the story is that if you want people to do things, you are far better to use a carrot than a stick. So if local authorities wanted care home owners to improve standards, the best way to do so would be to point out the advantages to them of complying rather than threatening them with punishment if they did not do so.

The presentation went down a storm with the audience. So tell stories. People love to hear them. They work.

Chapter Six

Rehearsing your speech or presentation

*'It usually takes me three weeks
to prepare a good impromptu speech.'*
Mark Twain

One of the keys to a successful speech or presentation is adequate rehearsal. And this may be a surprise to many of you. A lot of people - even highly experienced speakers - believe that rehearsals are not required and can make a presentation seem wooden and scripted. I would totally disagree on this point. It is well-rehearsed presentations that appear the most lively and spontaneous.

It is during your rehearsals for your talk that it really comes alive. You should do them with a stopwatch and pencil to hand. The stopwatch ensures you are not going over your allotted time slot and a pencil is needed to make amendments and corrections which may occur to you as you are rehearsing.

This is a principle that has been known for centuries. Abraham Lincoln (in the pre-typewriter era) used to carry around a handwritten draft of his next speech in his top hat. Any time he had a moment to spare he would take out his speech and a pencil, read it out loud and 'give it another lick' as he put it. Franklin D. Roosevelt's famous 'Day of Infamy' speech, which he made after the Japanese attack on Pearl Harbour in December 1941, started out as a much more complex oration which was then condensed down to a simpler form by repeated rehearsals and rewriting.

One of the worst mistakes you can make as a public speaker is to talk for longer than has been agreed. A surgeon who plans to take out three feet of intestine and ends up removing five is a bad doctor. Someone who is asked to speak for three minutes and ends up giving a five minute oratory is a poor speaker.

There is no excuse for talking for longer than the agreed time and it proves that you have not rehearsed your talk properly. Winston Churchill took six to eight hours to prepare a 45 minute speech. In her excellent book *Speak in Public with Confidence*, Maggie Eyre offers the following advice on this topic: 'Serious speakers need to set aside at least 45-60 minutes of presentation time per minute of speaking time. I spend at least one to two full days preparing for a one-hour speech and once spent four days preparing for a major speech'.

As I indicated in an earlier chapter, my favoured method for preparing speeches is to write down every single word I will utter. I then print out a copy in 14 point font size, double spacing (to allow room for pencilled notes and corrections) with consecutive page numbering, and then fit the resulting printed sheets into transparent poly-pockets which can be put in a four-ring loose leaf binder. This can be placed on a music stand for easy reference. My first few rehearsals though would be done with the consecutive sheets held together with a paper clip so that pencilled corrections can be made easily.

When you are rehearsing, read the speech out loud so that you get an idea of what the audience will hear. Ask yourself a number of questions as you speak:

- Have I expressed myself in as few words as possible?
- Have I written my script using spoken English? Are there places where I have inadvertently lapsed into written English?
- Are there points where a dramatic pause should be introduced? For example, a brief pause after a rhetorical question or before a key point can be very effective.
- Am I varying the speed and tone of my voice enough? Speaking in a constant monotone can be very boring for the audience but raising the speed and pitch of your voice can be used to denote excitement, while slowing down and deepening your voice can be used to signal the end of your presentation.

Most of your rehearsals can be done sitting down at a desk or table with a pencil in one hand, but your last two should be done standing up with your notes in a folder on a music stand. By this point the words should be very familiar and you should only have to glance at your notes occasionally, thus maintaining eye contact with the audience. I would recommend an absolute minimum of four rehearsals for the average speech, and if you can manage more than that then all the better. The more times you rehearse, the better your speech will be. I have been known to practice a talk as many as twenty times, even doing my final run-through in my hotel room just an hour or two before I am due to speak. If possible you should memorise the beginning and end of an oration, though committing the entire content to memory is usually impossible for anyone other than trained actors.

There is considerable scientific and anecdotal evidence that rehearsals really do aid your performance and I can give examples from other fields.

Back in the early seventies western governments were paralysed by a wave of terrorism, particularly the hijacking of airliners. They simply didn't know how to respond to what was happening. The nadir of this era was probably the seizure of several airliners (including a British Vickers VC-10) in September 1970 by Palestinian terrorists who had the aircraft flown to Dawson Field in Jordan where they were blown up in front of the international press. Around this time the standard response of western governments (including British PM Edward Heath's particularly weak administration) was to give in to terrorist demands: a policy which resulted in even more hijackings.

On 5th September 1972 a group of Palestinian terrorists infiltrated the Olympic village in Munich (an event which formed the core of the 2004 Steven Spielberg movie *Munich*). The West German government responded with a clumsy attempt to rescue the hostages. One of the many mistakes the German police made was that they did not allocate at least one sniper to each bad guy, something which would be standard practice in the British Army. The result was a debacle which resulted in the deaths of all the hostages.

Then in July 1976 something happened which proved to be a turning point in the battle against terrorism. On 27th June an Air France Airbus was hijacked by Palestinian terrorists and flown to Entebbe Airport in Uganda. Although many of the passengers were subsequently released, 94 Israeli passengers and six flight crew were held hostage in deplorable conditions in the old terminal building.

The Israeli government kept up the pretence of wanting a negotiated settlement while they prepared a military solution. On 4th July, without prior warning, 100 Israeli commandos landed at Entebbe Airport in four Lockheed C-130 Hercules aircraft. The initial strike force drove to the old terminal in a black Mercedes limousine and two Land Rovers, simulating the appearance of Ugandan president Idi Amin making an unannounced visit to his troops.

Almost total surprise was achieved. Every terrorist was killed, photographed and fingerprinted, and only three hostages died. The commandos then destroyed all the Ugandan Air Force's Mig-17 and Mig-21 fighters which were sitting on the ground and re-embarked all the troops, vehicles and hostages on the four Hercules aircraft which then flew back to Israel via Kenya, which had agreed to refuel the planes.

The effect on international terrorism was devastating. The number of aircraft hijackings slumped as terror chiefs realised that such undertakings were now likely to end with the deaths of all the terrorists involved. This point was rammed home the following year when members of the recently formed West German GSG-9 special forces (formed after the Munich debacle and based on the British SAS) stormed a hijacked Lufthansa airliner at Mogadishu in Somalia, releasing all the hostages and killing all the bad guys.

So why was the Entebbe raid ('Operation Thunderbolt') such a success? The answer was that the Israelis carried out a number of dress rehearsals to ensure that their plan would work. They obtained plans of the entire airport from an Israeli construction company which had built the new terminal and thus were able to build a plywood and canvas mock-up of the target which commandos practised on until they knew every inch of the actual building in Entebbe inside out.

There is nothing new of course about the idea of military rehearsals. The allies practised invading France (at numerous locations in England) for months before D-Day. And the SAS, at their base in Hereford, use a mock building called 'The Killing House' to practice rescuing hostages from a building held by terrorists, as featured in the excellent 1982 film *Who Dares Wins* and the superb 2003 TV series *Ultimate Force*.

'Mental Rehearsal' is a technique I used frequently in my work as a clinical hypnotherapist. After using methods to eliminate negative emotions, I would ask my client (under hypnosis) to see themselves successfully carrying out whatever it is they feared (which could be delivering a speech).

Rehearsals are also known to be vital in the world of showbusiness. Even the cast of long-running shows have been asked to start rehearsing again when their performances start to become flabby. The more you rehearse, the better your performance will be. As Clarke Peters once said, 'You need to make mistakes in rehearsals because that's how you find out what works and what doesn't'.

Chapter Seven

Delivering your speech
or presentation

'Good delivery will make
very thin matter go a long way.'
Dale Carnegie

So far I have discussed the importance of structure in a presentation, the correct way to script a speech and how vital it is to carry out some kind of rehearsal.

All of this is very important stuff, but it is of little consequence if your speech or presentation is poorly delivered. Powerful delivery really makes the difference between a good talk and a great one.

How many times have you sat at a conference, bored out of your box, listening to a speaker drone on and on in a monotone when all you really wanted to do was get out of the area as soon as possible? I am sure it is a universal experience.

So what then is the secret of good delivery? Here are some tips I have picked up over the years.

Feel some emotion about the subject you are speaking about

If you feel deeply about what you are talking about then that emotion will energise your performance. Admittedly this can be difficult when you are giving a presentation on loft insulation, but let's suppose you are speaking at a local meeting called to oppose the construction of an additional runway at the nearby airport. You feel angry because you know the whole project is motivated by money. You are irritated by the construction company who only want to make a big profit. You are annoyed at the bankers funding the project, who cannot lose. And you don't like the company operating the airport, who only want to bring in more revenue and don't give a toss about the views of the local population.

Building the new runway will involve the demolition of a small village. Local wildlife will be devastated. The extra noise and pollution will damage the environment. Feel that anger growing deep within you and then speak with 'fire in your belly'. It will make a great difference to your performance. As Dale Carnegie once said, 'Walk up behind the most inarticulate man in the world and kick the legs from under him, and he'll rise and make the speech of his life'.

I am a great fan of the James Bond books and films, and while I would agree with most people who consider that Sean Connery is the greatest screen Bond ever, I am also a great admirer of Timothy Dalton's performance as Agent 007. In preparation for the role Dalton read every one of Ian Fleming's original Bond novels and short stories and really got under the skin of the character.

The Bond of the books is really nothing like Sean Connery's interpretation of the role, brilliant though it may be. The literary Bond was frequently tense, anxious, worried, depressed and angry, and certainly never made jokes or uttered memorable one-liners. Dalton's performance is probably the closest yet to Fleming's creation as he infused his portrayal with great emotion.

How did he do this? Well, he probably used a technique known as the Stanislavski Technique (a.k.a. Method Acting) in which he recalled a time in his own past when he had a similar emotion to the one he wanted to portray and then thought of that incident when he gave his performance. Dalton is probably not a full-blown method actor, who tend to take things to extremes in their quest for a 'realistic' performance. During the making of *Marathon Man*, Dustin Hoffman supposedly ran for miles in order to appear breathless for a scene. Seeing this, his co-star Laurence Olivier quipped: 'Ever heard of acting, old boy?'

I would recommend that you watch Dalton's two Bond movies *The Living Daylights* and *Licence to Kill* on DVD or Blu-Ray, because they will give you a very good idea of how to infuse your performance with emotion.

Good examples of excellent delivery in public speaking can also be found in the 1955 film *The Dambusters* (at 65 minutes 54 seconds) in the scene where Richard Todd (as Guy Gibson) briefs his aircrews on the forthcoming mission. Another film scene worth watching is in the 1977 movie *A Bridge Too Far* (at 27 minutes) where Edward Fox (playing General Brian

Horrocks) talks to his XXX Corps commanders about their role in 'Operation Market Garden'. Horrocks' speech also contains a very powerful metaphor about Native Americans and the cavalry which is worth noting. Incidentally, Horrocks went on to become a 'TV general' in the 1960s and 1970s, presenting many programmes.

Introduce pauses into your speech

Many people have a poor delivery because they talk at a constant speed (often that of a fast firing machine gun) without any breaks. Pauses can be very effective in any speech, particularly before and after an important point or following a rhetorical question. Again, this is something that can be worked out during rehearsals.

Vary the pitch and speed of your delivery

Altering the speed of your talking can be a very powerful tool. Accelerating your speech rate can be used to denote excitement, while slowing down is an excellent way of denoting that the end of your presentation is imminent. Also emphasising certain words to make them stand out can be very powerful.

The late actor Patrick McGoohan had his own method of delivery which was almost unique but very effective. He would start off a line of dialogue slowly and in a relaxed mood but by the end of the sentence he would be shouting with anger, for example his memorable line of dialogue from the classic *The Prisoner* episode 'The Schizoid Man':

'Like growing a moustache....OVERNIGHT!'

Or this one from *Ice Station Zebra*:

'I want you to put another torpedo... UP THE SPOUT!'

McGoohan also varied the pitch of his speaking, a technique which can be very effective as a way of emphasising certain sections of a speech.

I would always recommend that you give your talk or presentation standing up rather than sitting down. The only exception to this rule might be a seminar or tutorial with a small number of people round a table.

Sometimes a lectern may be provided. I like them because they give you somewhere to place your notes without them being seen by the audience. My only concern about them is that the audience can only see part of you, limiting the way in which you can use body language to enhance your presentation, so it may be a good idea to step away from the lectern from time to time. If no lectern is available then I put my notes in their loose leaf binder on a music stand, making it easy to consult them as required.

Maintaining eye contact with the audience

Many of the characters in the 1969 film *Battle of Britain* were fictional, for legal reasons. However, some of them were clearly based on real people. For example,

Squadron Leader Skipper (played by Robert Shaw) was clearly based on the real-life South African ace 'Sailor' Malan.

Malan became famous for writing a document called 'Ten Rules of Air Combat'. The fifth rule is of particular interest to public speakers because it states that you 'should always turn to face an attack' and 'you should never turn your back on the enemy.' It is my contention that what applied to air fighting in 1940 is equally valid to public speaking in the 21st century.

In short, you should never, ever turn your back on the audience while making a speech or presentation. Yet I have seen people make entire talks like this. One particularly boring lecture I endured was done exactly this way. In order to work his laptop easily, the presenter placed his computer and data projector on a table in front of the audience. He then stood with his back to the audience while he gave a boring, monotonous oration.

Had I been asked to give the same talk I would have stood facing the audience, to one side of the screen, and worked the PowerPoint using a hand-held remote control so that I could maintain eye contact with the delegates.

When you give your presentation, stand facing the audience and with your arms hanging by your sides. You can then make any spontaneous gestures which occur to you. Always maintain eye contact with your delegates. With a small group, look at each person one at a time. With a larger audience, divide them into four quadrants and look at each in turn. Don't forget to look at the chairman of the meeting, and any other persons who may be seated to one side of you. If you have rehearsed your presentation correctly then you should only require to look at your notes occasionally, thus introducing pauses which can help your talk.

Coping with interruptions

It is my experience that some delegates always arrive late for presentations and conferences. Ideally they should then only be allowed to enter the room during breaks between speakers. In practice this may not happen, and these annoying people enter the hall rather noisily and are usually unable to find an empty seat. Similarly there may be interruptions when the caretaker arrives to open windows or turn off a noisy fan, etc. Under such circumstances I would always recommend that you 'pause' your talk until the disturbance is over.

In summary then, good delivery is vital to the success of any presentation. As Abraham Lincoln once put it, 'I don't like to hear cut-and-dried sermons. When I hear a man preach, I like to see him act as if he were fighting bees'.

Chapter Eight

Dressing for success

*'You cannot climb the ladder of success
dressed in the costume of failure.'*
Zig Ziglar

Another way to ruin an otherwise perfect presentation is by dressing poorly. When you are giving your talk you are under great scrutiny, whether you like it or not. People will make instant judgements about you based on your appearance and dress sense. Among other things they will observe is whether you have shaved correctly (if you are a man) or applied make-up in a flattering manner (if you are female). They will notice if your shoes are clean and polished, and whether your suit or dress fits you.

I would always advise wearing a dark suit while giving a presentation because this has been shown to be more commanding. This is the reason that politicians tend to wear dark (rather than light) suits. Men who appear in criminal courts are often advised (by their defence lawyers) to wear dark suits, a shirt and a tie because this tends to countermand the impression that might otherwise be made if they had appeared in their usual attire of shell suit and baseball cap. And research has shown that people who dress well for court appearances tend to get more lenient sentences.

Female presenters should wear a dark suit as well, although sometimes startling colours like bright red and blue can work for women.

Don't get me wrong. Most of the time I am a 'casual dress' sort of person who likes to slob about in tracksuit bottoms, T-shirt and clogs. At weekends, if I am not going out anywhere special, I don't even bother to shave. And in the summer months I find a shirt, suit and tie about as comfortable as a black bin-bag.

However, I have to accept that when I am giving a speech or presentation I am required to don the appropriate clothes to make the right impression, and this means a shirt, tie and suit. The only exception to this rule might be if you were asked to give a presentation to a small group of blue-collar workers. So for example if you were asked to talk to a number of oil rig workers or car mechanics at their place of work then you might want to dress in a similar manner to them to achieve rapport.

The usual rule though is that you should 'dress up' rather than 'dress down'. After all, how can you make a good impression if you look as though you have just spent the night sleeping on a park bench? I once attended a conference in Edinburgh and met one of my fellow speakers. He had shaved badly and had blood spots on his collar. He was wearing a striped shirt, gaudy mismatching tie and a checked suit. His shoes were scuffed and unpolished. He badly needed a haircut. And his gut was hanging out over his belt. I wasn't sure whether he was going to give a presentation or ask me for 10p for a cup of tea. I later discovered he was a Professor of Old Age Medicine. His lecture was terrible, incidentally.

Some years ago I signed up for a two-day training course in specialist hypnotherapy. Unfortunately the 'trainer' (if you could call him that) didn't adopt my favoured 'General Montgomery Approach'. There was no timetable, no plan, no lunch provided, and you paid for your own coffees. Worse still, there were no printed notes or manual. Everything just 'happened' spontaneously. How anyone would remember anything of the content of the seminar is a mystery. Worse still the 'trainer' was dressed throughout in a baseball cap, jeans and T-shirt and made frequent use of the 'F-word' in his presentations since he thought it gave him 'power'. How can you make a positive impression when you look and sound like a drug dealer?

So my advice to you all would be to dress well for presentations. Always wear a suit. Be immaculate, because immaculate people have special powers.

If you have not already done so, I would recommend you get a Personal Colour Analysis done by the 'Colour Me Beautiful' (CMB) organisation. See *www.colourmebeautiful.co.uk* for further details and a list of regional consultants.

The basic principle behind a personal colour analysis is that every person is one of four types - namely 'Spring', 'Summer', 'Autumn' or 'Winter' - and this diagnosis is determined by studying things such as the colour of the eyes, skin and hair. I had a Personal Colour Analysis carried out by a CMB consultant in 1990 and was found to be an 'Autumn'. This means (for example) that I should not wear pure white shirts when making presentations as these tend to drain colour from my face. An oyster white or pale cream shirt would be better. Similarly, jet black suits are not suitable for 'Autumns'. A dark navy blue colour would be best.

Whether you decide to have a personal colour analysis or not, you should be aware of colour combinations that go well together and those that clash. This is where women have the edge over men as they tend to be more aware of this issue.

A rule that I have devised to help you remember the colours that go well together and those that do not is the following:

> **Colour combinations that go well together tend to be those that are found in nature, e.g.:**
> - White and light blue (clouds against a summer sky)
> - Orangey browns and golds (a forest in autumn)
> - Brown and cream (flowers)
> - Red and green (many flowers)
> - Red and grey (winter sunsets)
> - Pink and grey (winter clouds tinged by low sun)
> - Grey and white (clouds)
> - Black and grey (snowy night)

- Black and white (low light levels)

On the other hand, colour combinations that are not found in nature tend to look 'wrong', e.g.:
- Blue (especially light blue) and brown
- Grey and brown

There are some general tips that I can give you for dressing. A patterned shirt should always be worn with a plain tie and vice versa. Or wear a plain shirt with a plain tie. A cream shirt with a dark red tie and dark grey or dark blue suit is a very good combination, often worn by politicians. You should never mix checks and stripes.

The colour of your socks should be the same as your suit or your shoes. Brown shoes should only be worn with a green or beige suit. Otherwise black shoes are the order of the day, and these should be in good condition and highly polished. 'Parade Gloss' polish is excellent for this purpose and used with a little water gives a mirror finish. Scuffed shoes are a no-no.

Your belt should be expensive and should be the same colour as your shoes. Some books on dressing suggest you should avoid clip on ties, but personally I like them as I was always dreadful at doing the knot on conventional ties. Clip-on ties always look perfectly knotted, plus you don't get the unpleasant sensation of having a noose round your neck.

Your hair should be immaculate. Men should visit the barbers and ladies the hairdressers.

All these things will give you greater self confidence: something that I will be dealing with in the next chapter.

Chapter Nine

Techniques for controlling anxiety and boosting confidence

'There are two types of speakers.
Those who get nervous and those who are liars.'
Mark Twain

Fear of public speaking (glossophobia) is a common anxiety, and this is the reason that many people refuse to give speeches or presentations. Yet this problem can be treated with a few simple techniques.

Anxiety prior to a performance is very common among actors and performers. Laurence Olivier, Adele, Barbra Streisand, Brian Wilson and Stephen Fry (to name just a few) have all admitted to having suffered from 'stage fright'. Curiously, the problem usually takes the form of tension before (rather than during) a performance. Fear during a performance is rarer, though it can happen. A common experience among both actors and public speakers is that they feel very stressed just before a performance but once this is underway the anxiety disappears.

A little bit of tension can aid your performance as the adrenaline makes your brain work better. However, full blown anxiety with a cold sweat and shaking hands etc. is clearly undesirable, and it is for this reason that I have listed a number of methods for controlling it, some of which I have used in my work as a hypnotherapist.

The Sarnoff Squeeze

The late Dorothy Sarnoff was a Broadway actress who became a public speaking coach. One day, as she was about to go on stage, she noticed one of her co-stars, Yul Brynner, leaning against the wall with outstretched arms. When she asked him what he was doing, Brynner explained that it was an anxiety control procedure that he had learned some years before. Sarnoff realised that this method worked because it caused the contraction of the *rectus abdominus* muscles, a vertical strip of flesh which forms part of a 'six pack'. Sarnoff hypothesised that the technique was effective because it caused some pressure on the adrenal glands, triangular structures situated on top of the kidneys which are normally responsible for producing adrenaline and noradrenaline, which cause many of the symptoms of anxiety.

This led Sarnoff to devise her own offshoot of Brynner's method, which is as follows:

1)   Sit upright with your back straight but not rigid, then lean forward slightly.
2)   Put your hands together in front of your chest with your palms together and your fingertips pointing upwards, and push.
3)   Say 'ssssss' as if you were a snake or a leaking car tyre.

4)   As you exhale while saying 'ssssss', concentrate on your abdominal muscles below your chest bone where your ribs begin to spread apart.
5)   Feel these muscles tighten as you exhale.
6)   Relax muscles and inhale slowly.

With practice you can learn how to do the 'Sarnoff Squeeze' without a chair, pushing your hands together or even hissing.

The Sarnoff Mantra
Dorothy Sarnoff's next major contribution to public speaking was the so-called 'Sarnoff Mantra', which is as follows:

Say the following silently inside your head several times before you are due to speak:
•   I'm glad I'm here
•   I'm glad you're here
•   I care about you
•   I know that I know

The Hara ('one point') Technique
This is a method I first learned from the great Paul McKenna at a 'Phobia Cure' weekend in London in October 2003. The procedure is as follows:

1)   Focus your attention on the spot one inch below your belly button and halfway between your navel and your spine.

2)   Now think of the situation you fear and simultaneously apply your concentration to that point in 1). Notice how much calmer you feel.

One advantage of this technique is that it can be used during a presentation without anyone in the audience knowing what you are doing.

The Spinning Technique
This was another useful trick I learned at the 'Phobia Cure' weekend in October 2003. It works as follows:

1)   Focus on the feeling of anxiety in your body. It should have a definite 'movement' to it. For example, a common pattern is that it starts in your belly and then moves upwards to your breastbone. What colour would you give to this anxiety? (e.g. red) And what colour would you give to the opposite feeling to the anxiety (relaxation or confidence)? (e.g. white)

2)   Now move your hand repeatedly over your body in the direction of the anxiety. So in the example above, you would be repeatedly brushing your hand vertically over your stomach and breastbone in a series of stroking motions.

3)   Now make that stroking motion part of a continuous circle which extends in front of your body.

4)   Now move that circle a few inches forward so it is outside your body.

5) Now reverse the direction of the movement of the circle and simultaneously change the colour from that associated with anxiety to the one you picked for relaxation (e.g. red to white).

6) Now re-install the circle and spin it faster and faster like the drum of a washing machine until all anxiety is gone.

Thought Field Therapy (TFT)

Thought Field Therapy (TFT) is a technique for treating a wide range of emotional problems which works by tapping with the fingers on various energy meridian points in the body. It was created by the late Dr Roger Callahan Ph.D., a Californian psychologist. In 1980, Callahan was treating a lady called Mary Ford who had a phobia of water (i.e. baths and swimming). Callahan asked her where she felt the fear and Mary replied that she felt it in her stomach. Callahan knew that the body's stomach energy meridian passed beneath both eyes so as Mary thought of the fear Callahan tapped beneath both eyes. Instantly Mary's fear vanished and has stayed away to this day.

Callahan repeated this simple technique with many other phobia patients and soon found that tapping under the eyes alone was rarely successful, but he knew that he was onto something and after a few years he produced his TFT 'algorithms': menus of tapping sequences which could be used to treat a number of issues such as trauma, stress, addictions, etc.

In this chapter I have given instructions on how to use the 'trauma algorithm', the most commonly-used TFT sequence, to treat both the past trauma of a bad public speaking performance and future anxiety about speech making.

To treat a past trauma about speaking

1) Think of the first incident which you think led to you developing a fear of public speaking. It might be an incident at school when you were asked to speak in front of the class. Rate how you feel **now** as you think of this incident on a scale of 1-10 where 1 is no anxiety and 10 is the worst it could be. This is known as the SUD (subjective units of distress) scale. If you cannot recall the first incident which lead to the problem, simply say out loud 'I want to be over the main trauma behind this problem' a few times and continue doing this as you proceed to step 2).

2) Now tap what is known as the PR (Psychological Reversal) spot on your non-dominant hand 10 times. This is the 'karate chop' surface on the side of the hand, halfway between the base of the little finger and your wrist.

3) Now take three fingers of your dominant hand and tap five times where the eyebrow meets the bridge of the nose (this can be the right or left side).

4)   Now take the same three fingers and tap gently on the cheekbone, an inch below the pupil of the eye.

5)   Now push your three fingers up into the armpit of the opposite side. Come down a couple of inches, about where the bra strap is in a female. Tap this point five times.

6)   Now find the collarbone point as follows. Feel the notch at the base of your windpipe. Go down an inch and to the right (or left) an inch. Tap here five times.

7)   Now find the 'gamut spot' as follows. Clench the fist of your non-dominant hand. Feel the point halfway between the knuckles on the back of the hand, corresponding to the little and ring fingers. Go back an inch towards the wrist. Now tap this point repeatedly while you do the following:

- Close your eyes
- Open your eyes
- Look down the right
- Look down to the left
- Whirl your eyes in a circle one way
- Whirl your eyes in a circle the other way
- Hum a few notes of a tune
- Count from 1 to 5
- Hum a few notes of a tune

Now repeat steps 2 to 5. Now recheck your SUD rating. If it is not a 1, repeat the process up to three times.

To treat an anxiety about speaking, think about a future speaking event then rate your anxiety on a scale of 1 to 10 and carry out the process described above.

If you want to find out more about TFT then I suggest you log onto the official TFT website *www.rogercallahan.com*. I would also recommend Janet Thomson's books on the practical application of TFT. Further details about TFT treatment points are shown at the end of this chapter.

Techniques for improving self-confidence

So far I have described methods for removing negative emotions. But what about installing a feeling of self-confidence during a presentation? To do this, I have recommended two methods from the world of Neuro Linguistic Programming (NLP).

The first of these is called 'anchoring', in which we set up an associational link between the desired positive emotion (e.g. confidence) and a physical action, in this case squeezing the finger and thumb of our left hand together. The procedure is as follows:

1)   Think of the positive emotion you would like to have during your presentation, e.g. confidence, enthusiasm.

2)   Now think of a time in your past when you had that very emotion. Close your eyes. See what you see, hear what you hear, feel what you feel. Make the pictures brighter, bolder and more

colourful. Make the sounds louder and clearer. Make the feelings stronger.

3) Now run through that memory again and again. Give the feelings a colour. Make the colour spread to the top of your head and from there all the way to the tips of your fingers and the toes of your feet.

4) Just before the feelings reach their peak, squeeze the tips of your thumb and index finger of your non-dominant hand together.

5) Now repeat the process four more times, using different positive memories each time.

6) Now squeeze the tips of the thumb and index finger of your non-dominant hand together as you think of speaking in public. You can repeat this technique just before or even during your presentation for maximum effect.

Another way you can gain the necessary confidence to speak well in public is by acquiring positive resources from another person. This is how you do it.

1) Think of someone who is a very confident public speaker. This could be someone you know; an actor, politician or celebrity, or even a fictional or historical character. Imagine they are standing in front of you. Notice their skin tone, their breathing, their posture. Now float out of your body and into theirs so that you are seeing

through their eyes, hearing through their ears, feeling through their muscles etc.

2) Notice how good it feels to be that person.

3) Now float back out of their body and into yours while taking these positive resources with you. Repeat this process a few times using different role models.

Using these techniques frequently will help you to become a better public speaker. As Rob Gilbert once said 'It's all right to have butterflies in your stomach. Just get them to fly in formation'.

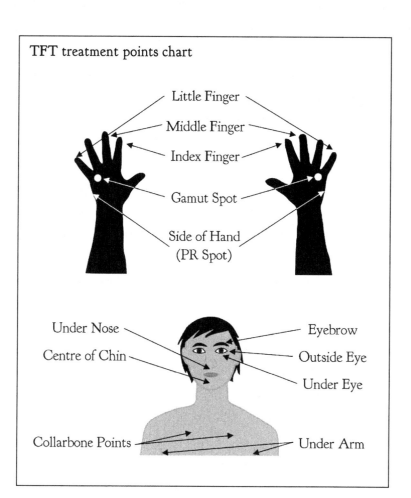

TFT treatment points chart

Little Finger

Middle Finger

Index Finger

Gamut Spot

Side of Hand
(PR Spot)

Under Nose

Centre of Chin

Eyebrow

Outside Eye

Under Eye

Collarbone Points

Under Arm

Chapter Ten

Using props in a presentation or speech

'Words may show a man's wit,
but actions, his meaning.'
Benjamin Franklin

The late, great film director Alfred Hitchcock once said that most films consist of 'talking heads' - which audiences find boring - and he always tried to avoid this in his own movies. He was right. All Hitchcock's films were carefully storyboarded in advance, in such a way that the story was told with pictures rather than words. If we take the famous shower bath murder scene in *Psycho*, for example, this was carefully constructed from a huge number of separate shots and meticulously edited together by the legendary Saul Bass. Many people who have seen the movie think that they saw Norman Bates' knife piercing Janet Leigh's body when this was merely implied. Incidentally, the reason Hitchcock made the movie in black and white was because he thought that the scene of Janet Leigh's blood draining away down the plughole would be too horrific: a restriction that would not apply today as evidenced by gory scenes in TV series such as *The Walking Dead*.

Hitchcock's comments apply equally well to speeches and presentations, because most of them consist of 'talking heads' and anything we can do to get away from the monotony of such a scenario is to be welcomed.

How would this work in practice? Let us say a certain official report came out recommending a course of action which you disagreed with. You might just say 'The Government should scrap this report'. Such wording would do the job, but it is not very memorable, is it? Better would be to say something like this: 'The Tories should rip up the report and toss it in the wastebasket'. That's a better way of saying it because at least it conjures up a dramatic image. But an even better way of getting the point over would be as follows.

Make up a fake report with an authentic looking title page and a plain back cover containing 20 pages of blank paper. Then stand in front of the audience and say the following: 'This is what the Government should do with this report!'

Then dramatically rip it up in front of the audience and throw it in a carefully positioned wastebasket. I actually did just such a thing at a conference more than 25 years ago. The effect on the audience was astounding. People almost jumped out their seats and I received a standing ovation. Incidentally, the only way you could top this visually would be by burning the report in front of the audience though this may not be a good idea in view of the current preoccupation with ''elf and safety'. Plus it would probably set off the fire alarms at your venue.

The practice of burning effigies of people you hate or the flags of nations you despise (which is always done outdoors) in some countries is based on the same principle.

On another occasion a few years back I was speaking at a conference, relating the tale of how I had once received a handwritten 'Dear John' letter in the post. At this point I retrieved a replica of the letter from my inside jacket pocket, tore open the envelope and waved the handwritten letter about. What an effect this had on the audience! Instantly my presentation became more memorable.

Before I go on any further, let's try this simple experiment. I assume that most of you have seen the original 1933 version of *King Kong*, which starred Fay Wray? Close your eyes right now and picture a memorable scene from the movie. Open your eyes. Most people reading this would have pictured the scene where King Kong stands on top of the Empire State Building and tries to swat down passing biplanes as if they were flies. Am I right?

The reason most people remember this particular scene is because it is such a bizarre mental image. People don't really remember words and phrases, they recall pictures - and if the image you present them with is unusual (or is achieved with a prop) then it will really stick in their mind.

About 20 years ago I did a personal development course called 'The Silva Method', and part of the training involved techniques for remembering names by converting them into pictures. The image for the name of one of my fellow delegates had to include the words 'man' and 'bicycle'. My Silva Method tutor suggested we all visualize a man standing beside a bicycle. But having already read a lot about this same subject (in *The Memory Book* by Harry Lorayne and Jerry Lucas) in the mid seventies, I knew a bizarre mental image would stick in the memory better. An image of a man standing beside a bicycle is simply too mundane.

I immediately suggested to my course tutor that the picture should be of a man standing beside a bicycle which was 100 feet high. He agreed that this would be more effective.

In 1975, when I first read *The Memory Book*, I learned a method for remembering numbers. The problem with recalling numbers is that they are hard to picture. However Lorayne and Lucas used a 'peg' system in which each number was converted into the sound of a consonant. For example 1 was 't', 2 was 'n', 3 was 'm', etc. I tried this out by taking a friend's phone number (which was 34439) and converting it to the right sounds, 'm... r... r... m... p'. I turned this into two words ⁃ 'mirror mop' ⁃ and then formed a bizarre mental image of my friend's house in front of a gigantic mirror. A huge oversized mop was sticking out of the roof, reflecting in the mirror.

Even today, more than 40 years later, when I think of my friend I see that bizarre mental image and remember his telephone number '34439'. Had I used a mundane visual image (e.g. my friend's house with a small mirror and a mop in front of it) then the method would not have worked. By the way, people have memorised entire telephone directories using the method I have just described.

So the conclusion of all this is that people don't really remember words; they recall pictures or actual objects. Using language which conjures up pictures is one way to make your presentation more powerful but even better is using appropriate props.

So if you are giving a talk on diets, don't just talk about chocolate: actually produce a bar, tear it open, let the audience see it and even sniff it. Incidentally, I always used to produce a chocolate bar when I was demonstrating how TFT could remove a chocaholic's urge. Then when you want to talk about healthy foods, produce some of them – such as bowls of apples and oranges. Unpeel a banana. All these things help to make your presentation more memorable.

If you are giving a talk on the Battle of Britain, have some models of Hurricanes, Spitfires and Messerschmitts to hand. Pick them up. Wave them about. I have my own word for this technique which is called 'physicalisation', where I actually produce the object I am talking about. If you are giving a lecture on techniques for overcoming fear of flying then have a large model of an airliner which you manhandle.

If you are giving a lecture on fishing then wave a fishing rod about. If you are talking about the joys of gardening then have a shovel to hand. Avoid being just a 'talking head'.

I gave the eulogy at my mother's funeral in 2014 and, at one point, I had to explain how she always spoke to ansaphones as though she was a Dalek from the BBC's long-running *Doctor Who* TV series. Not only did I mimic a Dalek voice at this point but I also produced a large model Dalek complete with appropriate sound effects.

Towards the end of my eulogy I also explained how, back in May 1973, my mother started to disco dance round the living room every time ELO's version of 'Roll Over Beethoven' came on the radio. That was funny in itself, but to make the point in a 'physical' way I played that exact music track on a portable CD and did a brief impersonation of my then 53-year-old mother boogying round the lounge. What a laugh that got!

On another occasion I used a radio controlled foot high Dalek to open my presentation at a TFT conference. This particular Dalek (the 'new series' version from the BBC's 2005 *Doctor Who* revival) had a voice function with six different words or phrases, each controlled by a different push button on the radio control unit.

This is how I used it :

CB: 'What words would you use to describe us TFT Practitioners?'

Dalek:	'We are the masters of Earth!'
CB:	'If one of the critics of TFT - the so-called "sceptics" - was to walk into this room, how would you respond?'
Dalek:	'Exterminate! Exterminate!' [sound effects of Dalek exterminator gun firing]

One of my friends and colleagues Michael Comyn, who is a well-known presenter and broadcaster in his native Ireland (as well as a trained TFT Practitioner), liked my opening but pointed out that I had taken a risk. What would I have done if my radio-controlled Dalek had failed to work? He was right, because there is a certain risk in using a high-tech prop which may go wrong.

The late John May once told a story about how he witnessed a prop misfire at a sales conference. The gag was that a rocket was supposed to run along a wire and then pierce a large paper bullseye target. Unfortunately things went wrong on the day and the rocket stopped halfway, showering some members of the audience with debris. A far easier way to achieve the same effect, as John pointed out, would be to have the presenter punch his fist through the paper target.

That is a very good point. High tech props can be very effective, but you should always bear in mind that they might fail to work and you should have a 'Plan B' ready just in case. Props don't need to be complicated or expensive, as I have already indicated.

I once opened a presentation by producing a universal container filled with 'urine' (actually apple juice). I then explained how nowadays a hospital laboratory could analyse this sample in minutes but 150 years ago doctors commonly tasted urine to detect various illnesses. At this point I put a finger into the container and tasted the urine. The audience recoiled in horror.

'That tastes not bad', I said as I proceeded to drink the entire contents of the container. Then I produced a huge plastic container marked 'Extra Smelly Urine' and glugged back a huge quantity of the 'urine'. The audience roared with laughter as they finally twigged.

If you want to make the point that you don't like paperwork then noisily toss a box file into a waste basket. Not an original idea, by the way, because a similar scene appears in the classic 1956 movie *Reach for the Sky*.

It is not necessary for the speaker to copy exactly the examples I have given. Instead I would prefer if you understood the underlying principles behind the use of props and devise your own ways of using them.

Above all, avoid being a 'talking head' in order to make your presentation more memorable. As John May once said: 'No matter what you are talking about, if you can show it, do it, or demonstrate it as a model or even diagrammatically, your presentation will have more impact'.

Chapter Eleven

Using humour in presentations

*'They laughed when I said I was going to
be a comedian. Nobody's laughing now.'*
Bob Monkhouse

Used correctly, a little humour can enliven an otherwise mundane speech or presentation. When I was studying medicine at Glasgow University it was generally accepted that anatomy was the most difficult subject to learn since there was a vast amount of material to commit to memory, none of which was particularly interesting. Indeed, I have often said that remembering the entire anatomical structure of the human body is like trying to remember where every rivet in the *Titanic* is in relation to every other rivet. At the time I studied medicine, the most common reason for people flunking out of the medical course was that they simply couldn't pass the anatomy exams.

Paradoxically, anatomy was one of the best-taught courses in the whole medical course since the department had two excellent lecturers in the form of Professor Joseph Scothorne (or 'Joe Sco' as we used to call him) and Dr John Shaw-Dunn. Professor Scothorne spoke slowly and clearly with excellent delivery and diction, and drew excellent diagrams (using various colours of chalk) on the blackboard.

Dr John Shaw-Dunn, on the other hand, was renowned for his amusing and witty comments (he didn't recite 'jokes' as such), and his lectures went down very well. He was so popular with the students that he was elected honorary president of the Glasgow University Medico-Chirurgical Society in 1978.

So there is no doubt that a little bit of humour, correctly used, can make your presentation more enjoyable and memorable.

Having said that, I would be the first to agree that an otherwise excellent speech or presentation can be ruined by the inappropriate use of humour and jokes. One of my former mentors, John May, always said that his golden rule for humour was that if you are not a funny person in everyday life then you shouldn't try to be a stand-up comic when you give a talk.

I like to think that I am a humorous person. I used to draw cartoons and write funny pieces. When I was in my sixth year at Greenock Academy I even produced an 'underground' school magazine, full of cartoons and amusing articles which was read by my trusted friends. Only a single hand-drawn copy of each edition ever existed and I was never caught!

For that reason I have always incorporated humour into all my speeches and presentations. But that does not mean that funny material and jokes must be featured in a talk to make it interesting.

When I was studying medicine the Glasgow University Medico-Chirurgical Society did an annual 'members' night' at which students presented scientific papers. In 1978 and 1979 I did a couple of spoof presentations with the emphasis on humour. These went down very well.

In 1980, the year after I had graduated, I returned as one of the judges. My fellow adjudicators were Professor Kenneth Calman (later to become the Chief Medical Officer and father of the comedian Susan Calman) and Mr Sam Galbraith (then a neurosurgeon but much later an MP and Government minister).

One of the contestants had clearly witnessed my performance during the previous two years, because he appeared to be attempting something similar. He certainly looked good in a tuxedo as he announced that he was going to give us his 'observations' on the medical course.

Unfortunately almost all his material was extremely unfunny and he didn't get a single laugh. For example, one of his 'jokes' was that when you were using an ophthalmoscope you had to look through the right side or you wouldn't see anything. Hilarious, eh?

The only decent joke in his whole routine was an old one, well known in medical circles: 'Neurotics build castles in the air, psychotics live in them, psychopaths blow them up, and psychiatrists collect the rent'. Unfortunately he blew the joke completely by presenting the different elements in the wrong order as Sam Galbraith was quick to point out.

I was literally clenching my buttocks in embarrassment. That man 'died' more times than Captain Jack in *Torchwood*. It was an abject lesson on how not to use humour in a presentation.

My late father (a GP) was what might be described as an 'unconscious comedian'. He used to do and say things that were extremely funny, without realising it. But he wasn't good at remembering or delivering jokes, and had difficulty understanding any kind of humour that was the least bit *avant garde*. I recall him standing in front of the television while I was watching *Monty Python's Flying Circus* with my brother Alastair. My father simply couldn't understand the humour.

The late Margaret Thatcher was a bit like that, as she was renowned for her lack of humour. When told about *Monty Python* she supposedly said 'Monty Python? I have never heard of him. Is he funny?' Her speeches tended to be very serious and when they incorporated witticisms they were written by someone else, usually Sir Anthony Jay who had scripted the popular BBC TV series *Yes Minister*. A good example would be her well known 'The lady's not for turning' speech in which she refuted the idea that there might be a U-turn in her policies: 'U turn if you want to; the lady's not for turning'.

So what then makes a good joke? It is often said that dissecting a joke is a bit like dissecting an animal. Both die in the process. Many people believe they have a 'good' sense of humour. Indeed, GSOH (Good Sense of

Humour) is one of the most common claims made in 'blind dating' websites, though in practice such people are more likely to have NSOH (No Sense of Humour).

So what then is a 'good sense of humour?' I don't know. And if there is really such a thing as a 'good' sense of humour then there must also be such a thing as a 'bad' sense of humour. What is that? I have no idea.

I think in reality there is no such thing as a 'good' sense of humour. It is more that we tend to laugh at jokes which mirror our own personal experiences. We identify with them. In the world of Neuro Linguistic Programming (NLP), there is a concept that we all have an inner 'map of the territory' and that everyone has a slightly different map.

I believe that the skill of great comedians is that they come up with observations which reflect our own experiences of the world we live in. Billy Connolly (arguably a 'comedy god') is the master of humorous observations of everyday experience, e.g. 'Have you ever noticed that every time you are sick there is diced carrot in the vomit? But I never eat diced carrot.'

I also remember Connolly reciting a tale of what it was like to go to public swimming baths in Scotland in the early sixties. He remembered seeing young men wearing home-made woollen swimming trunks with a tiny pocket on the front. What was the pocket for? I found that remark extremely funny because it coincided with my own personal experience.

The brilliant Alexei Sayle once did a superb gag about 'the first law of mechanics' which was as follows:

'The First Law of Mechanics. Can't fix that mate. Ooh... can't fix that. Got to get the parts in from Nair... obi.'

This made me laugh because we have all had the experience that our car, TV, washing machine etc. can't be repaired due to the fact that a certain spare part is not available. I was once told that my 5-year-old SHARP DVD recorder couldn't be fixed because spare parts were no longer available. The first law of mechanics again.

(By the way, in reality the 'First Law of Mechanics' comes from the work of Isaac Newton and refers to the fact that an object will either remain stationery if no force is applied to it, or else travel at a constant speed when force is applied.)

All humour has anxiety at its core. We tend to laugh at things that make us anxious. That is why jokes about sexual activities and toilet functions are so popular and apparently so funny. It is not that these activities are intrinsically risible in themselves, it is more that we all have anxieties about them and where there is anxiety there is humour. In fact, many sexual jokes have a very simple structure to them; similar to childish jokes, but the subject matter - sexual intercourse and all the anxieties which surround it - make them seem sophisticated.

Most jokes have the same basic structure which can be summarised as follows:

'It is not X it is Y.'

In other words, we lead the audience down a certain path and then – contrary to the expectations that have been built up – we reveal that we are talking about something else.

For the joke to work, the realisation that 'it is not x it is y' should occur at the last possible moment: ideally the final word of the joke. Let me give you an example, from an early episode of *Monty Python's Flying Circus*:

'My dog's got no nose.'
'How does he smell?'
'Terrible.'

The joke works because it based on the two possible meanings of the word 'smell', and the realisation that 'it is not x it is y' occurs in the very last word of the joke. This is a very important point, as the exact wording of the joke and the order in which the individual components are delivered makes all the difference. So if the joke is delivered in such a fashion that the realisation that 'it is not x it is y' occurs well before the end of the joke, it can cease to be funny.

The late Bob Monkhouse gives a very good example of this in his excellent book *The Complete Speaker's Handbook: Just Say a Few Words*.

Comedian Jack Douglas made an after-dinner speech at a formal banquet, at which he was preceded by two long-winded speakers who simply would not shut up. This is how Douglas opened his speech:

'Mr Chairman, what a great dinner. If I'd known it was going to run this long I'd have *bought* the dinner suit.'

As Monkhouse pointed out, it is funny because of its construction. If Douglas had said 'I wouldn't have hired this suit if I'd known the dinner was going to run this long' then it wouldn't have been funny. So the exact construction of the joke is vital.

A joke should also be appropriate for the occasion. One of the most common faults I have observed in 40 years of listening to other peoples' speeches is that the jokes used are funny but don't match the topic of the presentation. So if you are giving a talk to a group of doctors then use a few medical jokes. If you are talking about slimming then have a few jokes about the difficulties some people have losing weight, e.g. 'I'm on the seafood diet. I see food and I eat it'.

I once saw the great comedian Griff Rhys Jones making a gag about Einstein's theory of relativity: 'Relativity, the discovery without which Christmases would be much more enjoyable'. I loved the joke which coincided with my own views on irritating relatives. I liked it so much, I even used it in a speech I made to the residents at Ashlea Nursing Home. However, it didn't get a laugh on that occasion and I think the reason was that people who live in nursing homes like relatives to visit them ⁓ particularly at Christmas ⁓ and don't find them the least bit annoying.

One of my friends once told me a joke about a WW2 flying ace recounting his experiences:

'There were Fokkers to my right and Fokkers to my left.'
'Wow.'
'Yes and some of them were Messerschmitts.'

That joke never worked for me. It is based on the fact that the words 'fokkers' and 'fuckers' sound similar, but also on the assumption that the 'Fokker' was a German aircraft. As any aviation enthusiast (such as myself) will point out, the Germans did indeed use Fokker aircraft in WW1 (such as the famous DR1 Triplane flown by 'The Red Baron') but in the 1939-45 conflict Fokkers were Dutch aircraft which fought *against* the Germans. So that joke might go down well with a general audience but would not be suitable for a group of aviation enthusiasts.

Ben Elton once did a joke which was about the 'superconductivity' of teapots in motorway service station restaurants. He was referring to the fact that they appear to conduct the heat of the fresh tea inside them with great efficiency, causing you to burn your hands. That joke never worked for me because the term 'superconductivity' actually refers to much lower electrical resistance at very low temperatures. So the exact context in which you tell a joke can be vital.

My late father (a GP) had little experience of public speaking, and felt very nervous at the prospect of making a speech at my sister Sally's wedding in July 1974. However, he was determined to do his best and had a typed copy of the speech sellotaped next to his shaving mirror for weeks beforehand.

My father decided to top and tail his speech with a joke. This is how he opened his talk:

'Ladies and Gentleman, I am a member of the medical profession and - as my duty is to relieve suffering, not inflict it - my speech will be brief.'

I thought this was a really good opening. In fact I have used it myself a couple of times. As well as being funny, it lets the audience know the speech is going to be short: something which they will appreciate.

He then ended his speech with the following joke:

'After the Six Day War in 1967, an American general asked his Israeli counterpart how his numerically inferior forces triumphed over the Arab armies which surrounded his country. He thought for a moment and then replied: "My men are all good businessman. When they charge they overcharge".'

Quite a good joke. The only criticism I would make is that the topic doesn't quite match the scenario of two people getting married.

If you don't know any good jokes yourself then you can get them from suitable reference books. For example, Bob Monkhouse's book on public speaking contains many jokes for different occasions and there are a number of other volumes on the subject. (Full details can be found in the 'Further Reading' section at the end of this book.) Nowadays it is also possible to get suitable jokes for free on the Internet.

Another tip I have picked up over the years is this: always attribute a funny joke or amusing quotation to a well-known comedian such as Groucho Marx or Woody Allen. This will result in it getting a greater laugh.

For example, if I was to make the following joke it might get a few titters:

'Mixed emotions. That's what you feel when you see your mother-in-law reversing over the cliff in your new car.'

However if you were to preface the joke with the words 'As the late Les Dawson once said...', it will get a much better laugh. When you attribute a joke to a famous comedian then people feel they are expected to laugh uproariously. So they do.

Another important point is that you should not use jokes (and humorous observations) which offend members of the audience. Here the context can be vital. So an anti-Tory joke which might go down a storm at a Labour Party or TUC Conference might not be so well received at a gathering of diplomats overseas.

For this same reason jokes about disabilities, race and homosexuality which might have been commonplace in the 1970s are no longer acceptable to modern audiences. Incidentally, you might not think that uttering the words 'getting down to the nitty gritty' would be racist, but apparently some people in local government consider it to be so since this term was once used to describe the detritus left on the lower decks of slave ships when they discharged their human cargoes.

Having said that, it must be recognised that the pendulum has perhaps swung too far in the opposite direction when it comes to humour. Some local councils have even sent circulars to their staff warning them not to make jokes in the workplace since many of them are 'racist, homophobic and offensive to people in certain ethnic groups'. The words 'black coffee' have even been banned in some local council offices as it is deemed offensive. Apparently the words 'non-white coffee' should be used instead.

So make appropriate use of humour in your presentations. As Herbert Gardene said: 'Once you get people laughing, they're listening and you can tell them almost anything'.

Chapter Twelve

Using visual aids

'If God is in the details,
then the Devil is in PowerPoint.'
Paul Rand

Visual aids can greatly enhance a presentation, but in my personal experience they are often used incorrectly, resulting in extreme audience boredom or 'Death By PowerPoint' as it is otherwise known.

So one important question you need to ask yourself is whether visual aids are really needed. Many an otherwise excellent speech or presentation has been ruined by a superfluous PowerPoint. When I gave the eulogy at my mother's funeral in May 2014 I briefly considered using a laptop and data projector to display pictures. Eventually I decided to eschew PowerPoint as the risk of a technical failure (bearing in mind the very limited set-up time I had) was so high. To display visual material I used instead the old-fashioned method of blowing up an image on a photocopier and pasting it to a large rectangle of coloured foam board, which I could display at the appropriate moment. Very low-tech, but very effective. I will be discussing PowerPoint in greater detail later in this chapter, but first I would like to describe other visual aids.

Blackboards

When I was at school (1961-1974) the blackboard was the main visual aid, and some teachers became very skilled in its use. It is actually very difficult to write and draw clearly using chalk on a blackboard and, as this particular device is almost obsolete, I will say no more about it.

Whiteboards

These have effectively replaced the blackboard and are much easier to use and clean. They are only really of use for small group seminars, not lectures with large audiences.

Flip charts

These have the same advantages and disadvantages as a whiteboard. One problem is that it can sometimes be difficult to write neatly, keeping lines of text straight. This problem can be avoided by lightly sketching in guide lines, or even text, using a pencil prior to your presentation.

Epidiascope

This invention dates back to the early 19th century and is effectively a device for projecting an image from opaque media (such as a photographic print) onto a screen. It was superseded by the overhead projector which uses images on transparent acetate film.

Overhead projector

The first overhead projector was produced in the 1870s, but they didn't really take off till the late 1950s. They should now be regarded as obsolete as they have been effectively replaced by PowerPoint.

35mm slides

These were very popular for presentations in the 1970s and 1980s. Colour slides taken with a 35mm camera could be displayed, as could lettering, particularly the dreaded (and highly soporific) 'white lettering on blue background' slides which were all the rage in the 1970s. The main snag of 35mm slides was that they required the room to be plunged into darkness, making note-taking impossible. On the other hand, this did help you to catch up on your sleep!

Using models (miniatures)

Any type of model can be used to great effect during a presentation, and I have already touched on this topic in a previous chapter concerning the use of props. For example, if you are talking about a proposed housing development, have a large model of it near you as you talk. If you are speaking about the moon landings have miniatures of the Apollo spacecraft. Pick them up and play with them.

A model which actually 'works' is even better. So if you are talking about a particular type of car, bring along a radio-controlled toy version which scoots along the floor, lights flashing and horn tooting. If you are speaking about steam engines have a Mamod traction engine in front of you. Fire up the engine and let the audience see, hear and smell a steam engine in action.

PowerPoint

The main visual aid used nowadays in presentations is PowerPoint. First developed for Apple Mac computers in 1987, it was subsequently purchased by Microsoft for use with its operating systems and launched in 1990.

It has a number of advantages over previous visual aids, as people with little experience or training can produce their own high quality slides relatively quickly. Colour photographs (whether taken by a digital camera or scanner) can be added to PowerPoint slides, as can photos sourced from the Internet. It is even possible to do complete slideshows of pictures, show movie clips, and add sound effects. Also, PowerPoint presentations can be shown under normal lighting conditions.

Unfortunately there are a number of snags to PowerPoint presentations which I have identified. First of all, since the slides are easy to prepare there is a great temptation to put vast amounts of information on each slide and for huge numbers of slides to be used: the dreaded 'Death By PowerPoint'. I have seen whole novels up there on the screen!

I once witnessed a presenter put every single word of her 45-minute talk on a series of PowerPoint slides. She then stood with her back to the audience and read the words off the screen. At one point she even managed to get between the projector and screen, resulting in the words being projected on her back.

Astonishingly, the conference chairman described her presentation as 'captivating' - which just goes to show that one quality you need to chair a conference successfully is to be a good liar. It is no wonder that many convention MCs end up in politics!

Another common mistake is to have too many bullet points on each slide, and an excessive number of words in each bullet point. There is a remedy which is known as the 4x4 rule i.e. no more than 4 bullet points per slide, no more than 4 words per bullet points. Some people use instead the 5x5 rule or the 6x6 rule. Certainly I would recommend that you have no more than 6 bullet points per slide and no more than 6 words per bullet point, and - if you can get away with less bullet points and less words - so much the better. If you do need to have more than a few bullet points then the solution is to have the information spread out over two or more slides.

So a practical application of these principles would be a slide which looks like this:

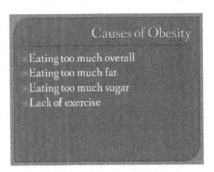

You will notice I have used only four bullet points, and no more than four words per bullet point. However, there is still a problem with this slide because I have revealed all of the bullet points in one go. A far more effective way of imparting the same information would be as follows. First you reveal just the headline:

Then, with a click on your remote, you reveal the first bullet:

Click again to reveal the next bullet point:

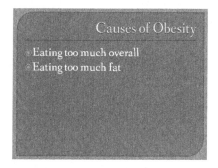

Click again to reveal the next bullet point:

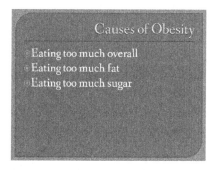

Click again to reveal the next bullet point:

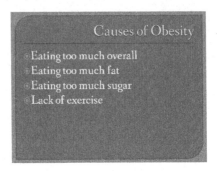

Thus each bullet point is revealed one at a time. There are two ways of doing this. One method involves producing a single slide with all of the bullet points included, then employing the animation features of PowerPoint so that each click of the remote reveals one bullet point after another. Each point is displayed with a fade, wipe, or some other effect. The other way of doing it, though arguably a more convoluted method, would be to set up consecutive slides which contain increasingly more information as the presenter advances through them. This is done by duplicating the items on each previous slide into the next (first only the title, then the initial bullet point, then the second, etc.) until all of the information is gradually displayed by clicking through the different slides one by one.

The technique of revealing one bullet point at a time has been used in television for decades. It is very powerful. Yet how many people use it in their presentations? Almost no-one in my experience.

Another bad mistake is to scan a complete page of a complicated textbook into a PowerPoint and then project the image on the screen. No-one will be able to read it, and it will distract the audience. They will try to read what's on the slide, attempt to make notes and fail, and while this is all happening they won't be listening to what you are saying.

When you are giving a PowerPoint presentation, always stand in front of the audience to one side of the screen and operate your laptop (and hence your slides) using a hand-held wireless remote control. Don't look at the screen and read what's on it. If you need to see what's on the slide you are using set up your laptop so you can see a small version of your slides while maintaining eye contact with your audience. Don't give your presentation standing behind the data projector or the audience, since you will simply become a disembodied voice. The only exception to this rule might be a lengthy video presentation which you talk over.

PowerPoints have another snag which is that there is a facility to produce 'PowerPoint Workbooks': essentially a hard copy printed version of the PowerPoint presentation. In my opinion this is a very lazy way of producing a handout or set of notes. If the presentation was rubbish then the workbooks will be terrible as well. A far better idea is to produce proper printed handouts, a subject I will deal with in the next chapter on speaking at conferences.

Right and wrong ways to present data

Wrong

One of the most important considerations in these clinical trials is that of comparing the effect of the drug on patients' pulse rate over time.

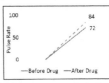

As the above graph indicates, the test participants who had not received the drug demonstrated an average pulse rate of 84 bpm, whereas those to whom the drug had been administered gave an average reading of only 72 bpm. This is clearly a very marked difference, and the results suggest the effectiveness of this new drug even after a short period. Further trials have been recommended in the near future.

Right

Effect of Drug on Pulse Rate

Before Drug

84

After Drug

72

Chapter Thirteen

Speaking at conferences

'The world is waiting for your words.'
Arvee Robertson

As a proficient public speaker you may be asked to talk at a conference, or organise the event, or chair it - sometimes all three - so it is very important that you know how to perform these tasks.

As the Scottish Chairman of the British Federation of Care Home Proprietors (BFCHP) 1985-91, and then as a founder member and chairman of the Scottish Association of Care Home Owners (SACHO) 1991-99, I was involved in organising, chairing and speaking at a large number of conferences. I have also arranged two of the conventions run by the British Thought Field Therapy Association (BTFTA) and was a speaker at four of them, so I would say I have a fair experience of such events.

Organising a conference

The first step in organising a conference is to pick a suitable venue. I would always choose somewhere that is easy to get to, whether by car or by public transport. You should not assume that everyone can drive to the conference. I once attended a conference which was in the middle of nowhere. The conference organiser chose the venue because it was close to where he lived. Although it was highly convenient for him, it was very difficult to get to if you didn't live locally. It cost me several hundred pounds to attend this one-day event, because I had to stay two nights in a hotel and travel to and from the nearest airport in a highly expensive taxi as there were no train services in that part of rural England.

If I was organising a conference in Scotland, I would choose a venue in Glasgow or Edinburgh. If I was setting up one in England I would go for London. Rather paradoxically, it can be cheaper and easier to travel from where I stay (Dunblane, near Stirling) to London than it is to go to locations such as Birmingham or Manchester. Conference venues in central London can be expensive, but you can get good deals if you choose cheaper venues such as private clubs. Another option is to use a hotel near one of the London airports, which can be much less expensive than similar venues in the city centre. I have organised two conferences at one of the Premier Inns near Heathrow Airport and found the accommodation and food to be reasonably priced and of good quality.

A site visit is essential. Among other things you need to check if the room is a suitable size, has good acoustics, and is well ventilated. Air conditioning is a must nowadays, and you need to ensure that this can be switched on without producing unacceptable noise. You should also bear in mind that your conference room will tend to get much warmer when there is an audience present, as all the bodies will heat up the room.

For that reason I avoid holding conferences or training seminars in the summer months, as the room may be too hot. I recall attending a training event in London in June 2004. Even though the room had air conditioning, it simply couldn't cope with the heatwave conditions and delegates were soaked in sweat. I also avoid holding conferences in the winter as the chance of people being unable to attend due to adverse weather conditions is so high. My personal preference therefore is to hold such events in the autumn or spring.

The usual seating arrangement for conferences is theatre-style. If possible, seats should be arranged so that people in each row can see through the gap between the heads of the people in the row in front of them.

Speaker liaison

Once you have decided the theme of your conference and have chosen your speakers, it is important that you give them as much information as possible about what will be required of them. In particular, speakers must be given full details of where and when the conference is to be held, the timetable for the day, details of the other speakers, the topics to be discussed, and how to get there by car or public transport as well as the arrangements for car parking.

There should be a detailed discussion about the content of their presentation and its length. My own preference is to allocate each speaker a slot which is exactly the same length. This might be 45 minutes broken down to 25 minutes for the talk and 20 minutes for questions. The advantage of this method is that it is then a simple matter to swap speakers' slots without affecting the overall timetable.

One thing I profoundly dislike are conferences which go on too long. I have witnessed such events starting as early as 8.30 a.m. and finishing at 6.00 p.m., or even 7.00 p.m. This is far too long. A 9.30 a.m. start is quite early enough with the conference ending at 4.00 p.m. or 5.00 p.m.

Several years ago I read about a two-day hypnotherapy conference which started at 8.30 a.m. and finished at 9.00 p.m. on the first day, followed by a formal dinner and then music and dancing which went on till 3.00 a.m. It was these long hours which put me off attending.

I have also heard of American NLP trainers who never have coffee breaks for delegates, deprive them of food and water, make them ask permission to go to the loo, and go on all day and all night in the belief that this is a 'good' thing. That is just weird!

Refreshments
When I have organised conferences and training sessions, I have specified a mid-morning and mid-afternoon tea and coffee break followed by a full one-hour lunch break at 1.00 p.m. A good three-course sit-down lunch is a must at conferences. I have been to conventions in which the lunch was 'rabbit food' served on paper plates and

which had to be eaten standing up, as no tables or chairs were provided.

PowerPoint

Not every speaker will use PowerPoint, but if they do then I suggest their presentation files are e-mailed to the conference organiser at least a few days before the event so that they can be put onto a single laptop which is then used for every presentation. A wireless remote control should be provided. I have attended conferences where every speaker brought their own laptop. Much time was wasted connecting each laptop to the data projector, getting it to boot up and the PowerPoint to work.

Microphones

Unless your conference is being held in a very small room, you will need to use a PA system and a microphone. Your mike may be fixed to a lectern or stand, or be hand-held. Another option is a wireless microphone, usually fixed to a lapel. If you do choose the latter option, check whether it is 'live' or not. I once had to make a presentation at a large conference in Edinburgh. I was fitted with a wireless mike which was not only 'live' but (unbeknown to me) broadcasting to the entire audience.

Just before I was due to go on stage I went to the loo for a comfort break, not realising that every word and sound I uttered was being heard by hundreds of people. Worse still, I needed not just a number 1 but a number 2. The audience was treated to a series of squelching noises, plops, farts and verbal utterances such as 'you can't beat a good shit!'.

When I got back to the auditorium I couldn't understand why everyone was roaring with laughter. Well, that's one way of breaking the ice!

The responsibilities of the chairperson

A good chairperson is essential to the success of any conference. Their main role is to open the event with a very brief introduction and then introduce each speaker. Speakers should never introduce themselves - this should always be done by the chairperson. To facilitate this, speakers should submit a brief biography (or even an introduction) some time before the conference.

The chairperson should also ensure that each speaker keeps to time. If the speaker has carried out sufficient rehearsals and timings with a stopwatch, they should know exactly how long they have to go. It is also a good idea to provide a clock which can be seen by the speaker so that they know that their allotted time slot is coming to an end.

Once the presentation is over, the chairperson can then ask the audience for questions. One potential problem is that some delegates will keep asking questions even after the allotted time is up. In such a case I would recommend that the chairperson simply states there is no more time left for questions. I have attended conferences with very weak chairpersons who have allowed questions to be asked well past the agreed time slot, which caused all sorts of problems such as tea and coffee breaks and lunch being delayed. Believe me, most conference delegates would rather have their lunch on time than hear the answer to a stupid question that should never have been asked in the first place!

Another problem that may arise at conferences is that delegates may ask questions during a presentation. While this may be acceptable in a tutorial or small group teaching session I would always recommend that in such situations the chairperson should tell delegates that questions will be answered after the presentation has concluded and not before.

I have also attended conferences where each speaker was required to sit as part of a panel during the entire duration of the convention, getting up to make their presentation as required. This is a very bad idea as the speaker will not get the full attention from the audience, who will be distracted by the presence of the panel members. Speakers should sit in the audience until they are required to talk. Once the chairperson has made the necessary introductions, he (or she) should leave the stage, only returning to take charge during questions. Thus during a speech the presenter should be the only person on stage, ensuring they get maximum attention from the audience.

Notes and handouts
When I was at Glasgow University in the 1970s, it was common practice for handouts to be given out at the start of some lectures. These were usually poor quality

photocopies of originals prepared on an electric (or even manual) typewriter. In some cases a handout would consist of a single sheet of A4 paper with headings on it. These were of little value. The better handouts were multi page and covered the main points of each lecture.

Although ostensibly a good idea, the problem with giving out handouts at the start of a lecture is that delegates will tend to read them during the presentation and not listen to what the lecturer is saying. A far better idea in my opinion is to give out such notes at the end of the talk.

Conference speakers can give out handouts in this way, but a far better system is to have a full set of bound notes - covering every presentation - which is distributed to all delegates at the end of the conference. Another alternative is to e-mail a full set of notes to every delegate after the conference or have them available for download from a website, a system which is used by many universities.

Any notes or handouts should be an edited version of the entire lecture converted from spoken English to written English. I don't like the current fad for e-mailing complete speakers' PowerPoint files to delegates or issuing them with PowerPoint workbooks, since these are usually incomprehensible.

Fees and expenses

Lastly we come to the thorny question of speakers' fees and expenses. At the very least the minimum package which should be offered to speakers is a 'thank you' letter plus a reimbursement of all travelling and subsistence expenses such as overnight accommodation, dinner, taxis, flights, train fares, mileage, car parking etc. Bear in mind that some people, such as local authority and NHS employees, may be able to claim such expenses from their employer.

You may also want to offer your speaker a fee. In some cases your speaker may ask for one as a condition of them making their talk.

I should add that in my 40-year career as a public speaker, there has only been a single occasion on which I was offered what I would consider to be adequate remuneration for my services. This was in 2002 when I gave a presentation about TFT to a group of GPs in Nairn, for which I was paid £300.

In my personal experience conference organisers can be very stingy, often going to great lengths to ensure that they pay you the minimum amount of expenses. In 2008 I was invited to talk at a conference in London. No fee was offered, but I was assured that my expenses would be met.

'I am quite happy to pay all your expenses', said the conference organiser.

Once the conference was over the organiser changed his tune saying that he was not going to pay my accommodation expenses as he could not see how I needed to stay overnight in London the evening before the conference. Eventually, after I produced his previous e-mails in which he had promised to pay all reasonable expenses, he relented and paid up.

I had an even worse experience the following year when I agreed to speak at a conference in Bournemouth. As soon as I had accepted the invitation to speak, the conference organiser did everything she could to keep my expenses as low as possible. As Bournemouth is difficult to get to from Scotland, I pointed out that I would need to stay three nights if she wanted me to remain for the entire event and two nights if I only stayed for the Sunday. On the other hand, if she was only willing to pay for one night's accommodation then I would only be able to attend on the Sunday for four hours before making my way back to the airport.

She decided to go for the last option. She also told me she wasn't willing to pay for any taxis, my mileage to Edinburgh Airport and back, my car parking, or my dinner the night before the conference.

I expected that I would be given a room at the hotel where the conference was being held, but two weeks before the event I got an e-mail saying that I was being accommodated in a cheap bed and breakfast several miles from Bournemouth. It wasn't the worst place I had ever stayed in, but it wasn't far off it. The tiny en-suite bathroom had a white WC and an avocado basin. The room was so small that the bed was almost touching the walls. The TV didn't work. I didn't get much sleep, as the next-door neighbours were holding a firework party which went on for hours. And the breakfast room featured an old bashed fridge (containing milk and fruit juices) sitting in the middle of the floor.

No taxi had been arranged to take me to the venue. Instead, the conference organiser turned up on the Sunday morning in a rusting, dilapidated 13-year-old Ford Escort. Its shattered bumper was held together with silver duct tape. I squeezed into this old jalopy beside some of the other speakers. All this had been done to save the cost of taxi fares.

I put many hours of preparation into my presentation, but I came away from that event feeling used and undervalued. Presenting at conferences may be satisfying and enjoyable, but in my own personal experience it is not a moneyspinner.

Chapter Fourteen

Being interviewed on television and radio

'The tongue has the power of life and death.'
Solomon

There is another aspect of public speaking which most books on the subject fail to cover, and that is TV and radio interviews. You may be asked to be interviewed about a book or report that you have written. Or you may even find yourself in the unenviable position of defending allegations that have been made against you or an organisation that you work for. It is therefore important that you know how to deal with these situations correctly.

I have considerable experience in this field. In the late eighties I was a nursing home co-owner and the chairman of the Scottish branch of the British Federation of Care Home Proprietors (BFCHP). At that time, private residential and nursing homes were attracting a lot of negative publicity. Much of this was actually instigated by a disparate group of people who I termed the 'anti-private sector lobby', made up of social workers, left-wing politicians, trade unionists and 'caring' organisations, who all enjoyed putting the boot into private care homes. Around this time, left-wing MP Harriet Harman authored a report entitled 'No Place Like Home' (which was funded by the trade unions) and focused on allegations of poor standards of care in some private care homes in England.

In reality what really bothered these 'do-gooders' was the fact that these private care homes were not run by the state and usually employed non-union members, something which the trade union movement saw as a threat to their own power base. In addition, the left-wingers who made up the 'anti-private sector lobby' strongly objected to the whole idea of people profiting from care of the elderly. The fact that the 'head honchos' in the NHS and Local Government were often paid huge salaries appeared to have escaped their notice.

Nonetheless, in the late eighties and early nineties there were a large number of highly biased and sensationalist TV documentaries such as Yorkshire Television's *The Granny Business* and BBC Frontline Scotland's *The Twilight Zone*.

The latter documentary, by the way, resulted in a case heard at the Court of Session in Edinburgh in 1999 which ended with the nursing home owners being awarded £186,000 in defamation damages. BBC Scotland also had to foot the legal bill which was estimated at £250,000. Judge Gordon Coutts QC said: 'The misleading inaccuracies are entirely the fault of the BBC and its inadequate checking of the alleged facts in its programme. The whole programme was unbalanced in tone, aggressive and contentious. They chose to use, without any reasonable proper checking, wild and exaggerated statements from disaffected individuals'.

There were also a number of poorly-researched and highly emotive newspaper features such as the series of articles in *The Sunday Post* in 1988 which made allegations of poor standards in some private care homes. One such article with the headline 'Smarties to make you Sleep' alleged that the owners of a certain nursing home were giving out 'Smarties' (sugar coated chocolates which visually resembled drugs) instead of sleeping pills to save money and make greater profits.

This was absolute nonsense, since the cost of such sedatives would be covered by each patient's individual prescription and giving out dummy sleeping pills instead of real ones (i.e. using a placebo) would be regarded as good - rather than bad - practice, something which I pointed out to a *Sunday Post* journalist at the time. Incidentally, the prescription of sleeping tablets to elderly people is now frowned upon as they can cause so many problems such as dizziness, confusion, falls and chest infections.

It was against this background of media hype against private care homes (which continues to this day) that I wrote a discussion paper on this topic for the BFCHP back in 1989. I pointed out in quite blunt terms that the reason we were getting such bad publicity was because our key officials were not trained in media skills as our opponents were. We needed to spend some time and money training our officers in such things as the correct way to write a press release, how to speak to reporters, how to be interviewed on television etc. My paper was well received, and one outcome was that it was agreed that the BFCHP would pay for me to receive some tuition on how to be interviewed on television. I had many practice sessions with Dr (now Professor) Peter Meech at the Department of Media Studies at Stirling University. Some of these were mock TV interviews which were video-recorded, and I told my interviewer (usually Peter) and another lecturer (playing the part of a loony-left social worker on a chat show) to be as nasty as possible to me so I would gain the necessary experience of such situations.

I also had a few one-to-one sessions with Professor Sam Black, who was then the recently-appointed Professor of Public Relations at Stirling University, and the culmination of my efforts was a conference on public relations skills which was held at the London Hilton Hotel near Hyde Park in March 1990.

Since then I have appeared on countless TV programmes and been interviewed on radio many times, talking about private care homes and (much later) Thought Field Therapy. I have therefore picked up many tips which I would like to impart to you in this chapter.

What to do if you are asked to appear on television

The first thing to do if you are asked to appear on a TV programme (or a radio show) is that you should find out as much as possible about the programme and more particularly the questions you are going to be asked.

Although you may believe that journalists are 'always out to get you', my own personal experience is that this is rarely the case. They are only really interested in making sure you perform as well as possible, and will do everything they can to help you.

Journalists will usually give you a rough idea of the questions that you are going to be asked. Even if they do not, you can usually guess ⁓ with a fair degree of accuracy ⁓ what these questions are going to be.

Then you should sit down at your computer and write down a list of the questions you are going to be asked (or think you are going to be asked). Then you write down concise responses to each question. TV and radio people like 'soundbites' of 15-20 seconds length, so you should aim to have very brief responses. If your answer takes four minutes to deliver then you may be edited down to 20 seconds if the programme is recorded. On live TV and radio the interviewer may simply butt in after 30 seconds to let another person have their say. You do not need to commit these responses to memory, but you should read them out loud a few times so they become familiar to you and you appear fluent while on air.

Another golden rule concerns anything negative that may be said to you. As Professor Sam Black told me in 1990, 'Never repeat any allegation that is made against you, and always reply with something positive'.

If the interviewer mentions something you don't really want to talk about (such as your failed previous marriage) then you should gently steer the conversation onto a more positive area. Also, don't introduce a subject you know nothing about as you will then be asked to say more on the topic. Thus you, the interviewee, controls the interview and steers it into areas you want to talk about.

You don't necessarily give answers to questions: you give responses, and you should have worked out well in advance what your main bullet points are going to be, regardless of what questions are actually asked.

Dressing for a TV interview

All the tips previously given on the chapter on 'Dressing for success' apply for a TV interview. Men should visit the barber the day before a TV interview, and women should make an appointment with their hairdresser. Stripes and checks on clothing should be avoided, as these may 'strobe' when viewed by TV cameras. Men should avoid wearing a bow tie as they will look like a nutty professor.

When you are being interviewed on TV, you should maintain eye contact with the presenter's eyes. People have a tendency to move their eyes around when they are thinking of the answer to a question. This looks bad on television as you will appear 'shifty eyed' and unreliable, so you need to keep your own eyes fixed on your interviewer's eyes. Never look directly into the TV camera.

Radio interviews

All the principles previously described for TV interviews apply to those carried out for local and national radio, except that you do not have to dress well for radio. Having said that, you may feel more confident if you wear a suit. It should be noted that some decades ago the BBC used to require its radio newsreaders to wear a dinner suit to read the news.

Chapter Fifteen

Miscellaneous speaking situations

'Oratory should raise your heart rate.
Oratory should blow the doors off the place.'
Rob Lowe as Sam Seaborn, *The West Wing*

After Dinner Speaking

I have done a lot of after-dinner speaking in the last four decades, particularly in my twenties when I was a junior doctor. The aims of an after-dinner speech are somewhat different to those of the usual presentation. People who have just had a heavy meal with wine, spirits and coffee are expecting to be entertained, not educated.

So making an after-dinner speech should only be contemplated if you are good at telling jokes and funny stories. PowerPoint, overhead projectors, whiteboards and flipcharts should not be employed. However, props such as models can be used to great effect, as can pieces of artwork on foam boards which you can display at the appropriate moment.

One of my favourite after-dinner speeches happened in November 1981, when I was asked to speak at the Glasgow University Medico-Chirurgical Society dinner and ball which was held in Glasgow University Union. I decided to do a humorous speech describing the life of a junior house officer using a series of props and pieces of artwork. To illustrate the poor quality of NHS food, I glued a fake vomit splash (obtained from Tam Shepherd's Joke Shop in Queen Street) to a dinner plate and held it up as an example of typical hospital cuisine. Some things never change!

I also produced a huge piece of artwork on A2 board which satirised typical GP referral letters of that period. At the top of the page I had the printed title 'Senocrap' then under that the words, 'increases bowel motility by 85%' and, beneath that, 'gives you big jobbies too'. The audience roared with laughter at this. A Glasgow or West of Scotland audience will always laugh at jokes about jobbies, willies, wee-wees and farts, particularly if they have had a few drinks.

Underneath the lettering (which was effected with self-adhesive vinyl letters), I had scrawled a very rough drawing of a patient's fat tummy (using a Magic Marker) with the words '? Abdomen, please see'. That got a good laugh, because at that time standards in general practice were not as good as they are now and junior house officers were often annoyed at the fact that some lousy GPs would send patients by the coachload to the nearest Accident and Emergency unit. When I worked at Law Hospital as a junior house officer in general surgery in 1979, we used to joke that the DDS (Doctor's Deputising Service) for out-of-hours home visits actually stood for 'Dangerous Doctors Service'.

I also produced a large model of a robot house officer (called a 'Robodoctor') which I had built myself from metallic card and pointed out its various features. That got a good laugh as well. You will notice how all the 'physical' things I did ensured that I wasn't just a 'talking head'.

The other speaker was a University Professor and his talk didn't get many laughs: something which clearly aggrieved him. I think the rule here is that ⁄ as the late John May once said ⁄ if you are not funny, you shouldn't make an after⁄dinner speech.

A couple of other points about 'after dinner speeches'. The problem with such speaking engagements is that you are being asked to talk under less than ideal conditions.

You will be giving your talk quite late, perhaps at 9.00 p.m. or 10 p.m. (sometimes even later) when you will be feeling tired. In addition, a heavy meal with alcohol and coffee is not the ideal preparation for doing public speaking since most of your blood will be down in your stomach trying to digest the meat and potatoes instead of flowing to your brain. Alcohol will diminish your performance, and coffee may make you anxious and jittery. So I suggest you pick at your food, don't have any alcohol and no more than one cup of coffee.

You should also ensure that you are at a top table so you can face everyone who is present and you don't have anyone behind you. Don't go on too long, and end in a punchy way.

Eulogies at Funerals

I have given just two eulogies in my entire career as a public speaker. I spoke at my father's funeral in 1996 and did the same at my mother's in 2014. In both cases, my parents had died after suffering from dementia for several years so their passing was more of a relief than a shock. My father was 77 when he died, my mother 93.

I adopted a similar approach in both instances, as I took the view that my eulogy would be a celebration of their lives rather than a commiseration. It should be noted that in the West there is tradition that funerals should be sad, solemn affairs whereas in some other cultures elsewhere in the world they are occasions for rejoicing as belief in the afterlife is so strong.

I started off each eulogy by summarising each parent's life and achievements. Then I went through their lives in greater detail, employing some humour here and there. I recounted some of my father's wartime exploits (as a Captain in the Royal Army Medical Corps), such as the time when he liberated a Belgian village single-handed after taking a wrong turn in his jeep 'thus establishing a penchant for navigational error which was to become a feature of our continental camping holidays in the early 1970s'.

I also mentioned an incident when a military convoy he was travelling in (in Normandy) was ambushed by a German Tiger tank, which used its 88mm main gun and two machine guns to completely decimate all the British vehicles. 'Did the British Army have a strategy for dealing with the Tiger tank?' I asked. 'Yes they did', he replied. 'When we heard one coming we all ran away'.

When I was giving the eulogy at my mother's funeral, I also mentioned an incident during WW2 which clearly affected her for the rest of her life. Her mother invited an airman in the Royal Canadian Air Force to come for dinner with the family. My mother did not say a word the whole night. As I pointed out (with my therapist's hat on), she seemed to be making up for that traumatic event for the rest of her life as she never stopped talking. As Groucho Marx once said, 'I've had many long conversations with her but I've never actually said anything myself'.

So that is the way I have done eulogies: with the emphasis on humour. Not everyone would agree. One public speaking coach recommends reading large amounts of glum poems, which wouldn't be my cup of tea. Unfortunately studying English at Greenock Academy from 1961 to 1973 put me off poetry for life, as the analysis of prose and plays was a very important part of the curriculum of 'O'-Grade and Higher English at that time.

Besides, I have never been able to take poetry seriously after seeing the 'Poet McTeagle' sketch in *Monty Python's Flying Circus*. In this comedy classic, a mean Scotsman's written requests for money are interpreted as brilliant poetry by the intelligentsia:

'Can I have £50 to mend the shed?
I'm right on my uppers.

I can pay you back
When this postal order comes from Australia.
Honestly.
Hope the bladder trouble's getting better.
Love, Ewan.'

Appendices

Appendix I

Improving your writing skills

Author's note: *This paper was first written by myself in the late eighties for the British Federation of Care Home Proprietors (BFCHP) and has been amended many times. It deals with written English, not spoken English, but most of the same principles apply although spoken English does not have to be as grammatically correct as written English. Proper sentences are not required in speeches and the principal of elegant variation does not apply either as repetition of a word or phrase can be very effective in oral presentations. I have also updated the list of clichés to take account of the latest entrants in this field!*

If you want to write good speeches and presentations then it is essential that you sharpen up your writing skills. **The difference between good prose and bad prose is like the difference between a sharp knife and a blunt knife!**

Almost everyone can improve their writing skills with a few tips and some practice. Unfortunately most people do not realise they are bad writers. In my own experience only a small minority of the population possess any skill at putting their words on paper.

Well-educated professional people are often the worst offenders, as they have slipped into a lot of bad habits over the years. In particular they often believe that 'good writing is complicated writing'.

In reality, as any journalist or editor will tell you, the reverse is true: 'good writing is simple writing'.

As Professor G.P. Duncan says in his book *How to Write Correctly*:

'The writer who adopts an easy flow is the one who deserves praise, not the one who refuses to call a spade a spade.'

In the next few pages I would like to point out some common errors in writing and ways in which they can be rectified.

Some Rules for Better Writing

1) Write in sentences and make sure each one has a subject, object and verb.

This may seem elementary, but it is surprising how often this simple rule is broken in reports and letters, e.g.:

'Regarding your letter. I have now studied it.'

In this extract, 'Regarding your letter' is not a sentence. (It is an unattached past participle).

2) Write using nouns and verbs rather than adjectives and adverbs.

Too many adjectives and adverbs can ruin a piece of writing.

3) Do not have sentences that are too long, as this makes comprehension difficult.

Novice writers are best advised to write in short sentences which can be joined together by conjunctions as required. It is equally wrong to write entirely in very short sentences as this can give your writing a staccato feel. Ideally you should have some long sentences and some shorter ones.

Sometimes you can make your writing more punchy if you join sentences with dashes (or semicolons) rather than conjunctions.

Compare these two examples:

1)   'His blood pressure was very low and this may cause problems in the future.'
2)   'His blood pressure was too low - this may cause problems in the future.'

4) Break your writing up with paragraphs. Start a new paragraph every time you introduce a fresh topic.

5) Do not use a complicated word when a simple work will do. For example:

Do not Write	If you can write instead
Purchase	buy
Quantify	measure
Issue	send
Communicate	write
Expectations	hope
Currently	now
Appropriate	right
Commence	start
Approximately	about

6) Similarly, never use three or more words to express something that can be said with a single word. For example:

Do not write	Write instead
Take action on this issue	act
In several instances	often
With the minimum of delay	quickly
In short supply	scarce
With the result that	so
On the occasion when	when

7) Always try to write in an active voice rather than a passive one. For example:

> Do not write:
> 'The conference was opened by the Health Minister.'

> Write instead:
> 'The Health Minister opened the conference.'

The reason that the active form is always preferable is that it is shorter and easier to follow. Admittedly, in the simple example given above, the meaning is not hard to grasp but it does make a difference when writing long passages of text which may be of a technical nature.

Sometimes the passive form is acceptable as a way of introducing some variation into your prose.

8) Avoid superfluous words. For example:

> *A complete monopoly*
> *The final conclusion*

This avoidance of superfluous words is a vital part of good writing.

9) Use concrete words rather than abstract. For example:

Do not write	Write Instead
Transportation facilities	lorries, cars
Entrance	door
Communications	roads, train
Communication	letter, postcard
Providing information	informing
In connection with	about
Your attention is drawn	please note
In conjunction with	with
Have in possession	possess

In each pair, the words ending -ition, ilities, or -nce are abstract nouns. The wording is more simple and vigorous if you replace them with concrete (= not abstract) nouns (lorries, cars, door, roads etc).

The reason that concrete nouns are preferable is because they can be pictured, and the meaning of the sentence is clearer. (You can picture a lorry, but can you picture a 'transportation facility'?)

10) Quotations should be used sparingly. Likewise avoid the temptation to keep dipping into foreign languages like Latin and French. This makes your writing hard to follow and impresses no-one!

11) It is inadvisable to repeat a word in a short passage, or to use close-together words that sound alike. For example:

Wrong:

'The new inspector, Mr Smith, has been appointed. The Inspector will be inspecting member homes in the Suffolk region and, after each inspection, will be making an inspection report which will be reported to central committee.'

Right:

'The new inspector, Mr Smith, has been appointed. He will be checking member homes in the Suffolk region and, after each visit, he will be compiling a report which will be presented to central committee.'

This is known as the principle of 'elegant variation'.

12) Avoid clichés. They devalue their prose.

Common ones to avoid using are:

* Absolutely
* Hit the ground running
* In meltdown
* A Perfect Storm
* A tsunami of...
* The tip of the iceberg
* The thin end of the wedge
* The greatest thing since sliced bread
* Between the devil and the deep blue sea
* By and large

- Broadly speaking
- At the end of the day
- When all's said and done
- Generally speaking
- Too little, too late
- Re-arranging the deckchairs on the *Titanic*
- Like a powder-keg waiting to explode
- Sitting on the fence
- Out of the frying pan, into the fire
- Shot himself in the foot
- A twin-track approach
- Iconic
- Parachuted in
- It's not Rocket Science
- You can take the girl out of Essex but you can't take Essex out of the girl (and similar constructions)
- Postcode Lottery
- We need a level playing field
- We need to touch base

That does not mean you should avoid interesting language which conjures up images in readers' minds, but rather that you should invent your own picturesque language instead of using some hackneyed phrase that has been used a million times before.

As Sam Goldwyn once said, 'What is required are some new clichés!'

13) Avoid using abbreviations except when absolutely necessary. They baffle readers. Jargon should also be given a wide berth.

Some people also have a habit of using words that do not even exist in the English dictionary (e.g. 'operationalise'), or use a noun as a verb (e.g. 'We need to resource it'). Always check in a dictionary if you unsure if a word actually exists, or if you are doubtful about its meaning.

Common Mistakes and Misconceptions

A lot of people believe it is wrong to begin a sentence with 'and' or 'but'. This is not true. Almost every page of Dickens has sentences beginning in this fashion.

It is also surprising how many educated people do not know when to use, 'Yours sincerely' and 'Yours faithfully'.

A letter beginning 'Dear Mr Smith' or 'Dear Peter' (i.e. where the name of the person is given) should always end with 'Yours sincerely', whereas if you start a letter with 'Dear Sir' (or Madam) then the letter should be concluded with 'Yours faithfully'.

Avoid using the split infinitive

For example:

Wrong
'He started to quickly walk down the road.'

Right
'He started to walk down the road quickly.'

Sometimes even experienced writers split their infinitives without realising it. Take this well-known piece of prose: 'To boldly go where no man has gone before'.

Another common mistake is the sentence: 'I acknowledge receipt of your letter'. You can acknowledge a letter and you can receipt a letter, but you cannot acknowledge receipt of a letter.

Sub Editing

Never submit a first draft for publication, even if it is a simple letter to the editor. Sit down with your first draft, pencil in hand, and study it carefully. Check that you have expressed yourself using the minimum number of words. This is essential.

Ask yourself the following questions:

- Are there any complicated words than can be changed to simple ones?
- Are my sentences too long?
- Are there any dull passive constructions that could be made clearer by converting them to the active form?
- Have I used enough paragraphs?
- Are there any words or phrases that can be omitted?

Often a bad piece of writing can be made presentable just by scoring out unnecessary words and phrases - newspaper sub-editors do this every day

Sometimes it is hard to spot errors in your writing, and the answer is to leave your draft for a day or two and then come back to it with a fresh mind. During the intervening period your subconscious will be working on the article, and you will probably find that you can write a much better piece of prose the second time around.

It is often helpful if you get someone to sub-edit your writing - he or she may spot errors you missed.

Finally, as an example of how a bad piece of writing can be improved I have reproduced below a letter which was sent to the *Sunday Times*. The original draft read:

'We are all aware of the significant need to maintain uppermost in the mind of mankind the stark need for avoiding bloody international conflict. One method by which this can be nurtured is to revive the solemn aspect of the great loss of life which has resulted from catastrophic struggles, within the theatres of war.

The attachment is associated with such an endeavour... I would appreciate a directive to your staff to review the attachment for the purpose of orienting this information so as to evolve a reasonably newsworthy article through your newspaper towards the end stated above.'

A *Sunday Times* sub-editor went to work on it, and the subedited version read:

Men need reminding of the horrors of war. One way to do it is to honour those who died and I would appreciate if you could use the attached information for a report on our ideas.

(Harold Evans, *Editing and Design: Newmann's English*, London, Heinemann, 1972.)

* * *

Further Reading

1) *The Business Guide to Effective Writing.* J.A. Fletcher and D.F. Gowing. Kogan Page. 1987. ISBN: 1-85091-292-2.

2) *The Right Way To Improve Your English.* J.E. Elliott. Right Way Books. 1975. ISBN 0-716-00505-0.

3) *How to Write Correctly.* Prof. G.P. Duncan. W. Foulsham & Co. 1975. ISBN 0-572-00180-0.

4)   *Using The Media.* Dennis McShane. Pluto
     Press.1979. ISBN 0-861-04089-9.

Appendix II

Further reading and resources

Speak Easy: The Essential Guide to Public Speaking
By Maggie Eyre
Exisle Publishing; 3rd edition, 2016
ISBN-10: 1921966858
ISBN-13: 978-1921966859

The Complete Speaker's Handbook
By Bob Monkhouse
Virgin Books (Reprint), 2012
ISBN-10: 075354055X
ISBN-13: 978-0753540558

Never be Nervous Again
By Dorothy Sarnoff & Gaylen Moore
Crown Publishing, 1988
ISBN-10: 051756 7091
ISBN -13: 978 0517567098

The Book of Days
By Bob Monkhouse
Arrow Books, 1981
ISBN-10: 0099271508
ISBN-13: 978 -0099271505

(This book gives details of what happened on a particular date in history.)

How to Develop Self Confidence and Influence People by
Public Speaking
By Dale Carnegie
Vermillion (Reprint), 1990
ISBN -10: 0749305797
ISBN -13: 978-0749305796

It's Not Rocket Science (and other irritating modern
clichés)
By Clive Whichelow and Hugh Murray
Piatkus Books, 2010
ISBN-10: 0749939737
ISBN-13: 978-074 9939731
(A funny book which highlights many modern clichés.)

Books on Thought Field Therapy:

Tapping the Healer Within
By Dr Roger Callahan and Richard Trubo
Piatkus Books, 2013
ISBN-10: 0749 941154
ISBN -13: 978 0749941154
Callahan Techniques website: *www.rogercallahan.com*

Tapping for Life: How to Eliminate Negative Thoughts
and Emotions for life using TFT
By Janet Thomson, MSc
Hay House, 2010

ISBN-10: 1848501889
ISBN-13: 978-1848501881
Janet Thomson's website: *www.powertochange.me.uk*

Paul McKenna

www.paulmckenna.com
Paul has produced many books, videos, CDs and downloads to
help people with anxiety and boost confidence.

Index

Y

Z

About the Author

Dr Colin M. Barron was born in Greenock, Scotland in 1956, and was educated at Greenock Academy (1961-74) and Glasgow University (1974-79) where he graduated in Medicine (M.B. Ch.B.) in 1979. He worked for the next five years in hospital medicine, eventually becoming a Registrar in Ophthalmology at Gartnavel General Hospital and Glasgow Eye Infirmary.

In December 1984 he left the National Health Service to set up Ashlea Nursing Home in Callander, which he established with his first wife Sandra and ran until 1999. He was the chairman of the Scottish branch of the British Federation of Care Home Proprietors (BFCHP) from 1985 to 1991, and then a founding member and chairman of the Scottish Association of Care Home Owners (SACHO) from 1991 to 1999.

Colin has a special interest in writing – his first non-fiction book *Running Your Own Private Residential and Nursing Home* was published by Jessica Kingsley Publishers in 1990. He has also written around 150 articles for various publications including *This Caring Business*, *The Glasgow Herald*, *Caring Times*, *Care Weekly*, *The British Medical Journal*, *The Hypnotherapist*, *The Thought Field* and many others. He was a regular columnist for *This Caring Business* between 1991 and 1999.

Colin has always had a special interest in hypnosis and alternative medicine. In 1999 he completed a one-year Diploma course in hypnotherapy and neuro-linguistic programming with the British Society of Clinical and Medical Ericksonian Hypnosis (BSCMEH), an organisation created by Stephen Brooks who was the first person in the UK to teach Ericksonian Hypnosis. He has also trained with the British Society of Medical and Dental Hypnosis (BSMDH) and with Valerie Austin, who is a top Harley Street hypnotherapist. Colin is also a licensed NLP practitioner. In 1992 he was made a Fellow of the Royal Society of Health (FRSH). He is a former member of various societies including the British Society of Medical and Dental Hypnosis - Scotland (BSMDH), the British Thought Field Therapy Association (BTFTA), the Association for Thought Field Therapy (ATFT), the British Complementary Medicine Association (BCMA), and the Hypnotherapy Association.

Colin has been using TFT since early in 2000, and in November 2001 he became the first British person to qualify as a Voice Technology TFT practitioner. He used to work from home in Dunblane and at the Glasgow Nuffield Hospital.

Colin has also had 40 years of experience in public speaking, and did some training with the John May School of Public Speaking in London in January 1990.

In May 2011 his wife Vivien, then 55, collapsed at home due to a massive stroke. Colin then became his wife's carer but continued to see a few hypnotherapy and TFT clients. In late July 2015 Colin suffered a very severe heart attack and was rushed to hospital. Investigation showed that he had suffered a rare and very serious complication of myocardial infarction known as a ventricular septal defect (VSD) - effectively a large hole between the two main pumping chambers of the heart.

Colin had open heart surgery to repair the defect in August 2015, but this first operation was unsuccessful and a second procedure had to be carried out three months later. On 30th November he was finally discharged home after spending four months in hospital. Unfortunately he also developed epilepsy while in hospital which meant he has had to give up driving for at least a year.

As a result of his wife's care needs and his own health problems Colin closed down his hypnotherapy and TFT business in April 2016 to concentrate on writing books and looking after his wife.

His interests include walking, cycling, military history, aviation, plastic modelling, and reading.

For more details about Colin and his work, please visit his website at: **www.colinbarron.co.uk**

For details of new and forthcoming books
from Extremis Publishing,
please visit our official website at:

www.extremispublishing.com

or follow us on social media at:

www.facebook.com/extremispublishing

www.linkedin.com/company/extremis-publishing-ltd-/

CPSIA information can be obtained
at www.ICGtesting.com
Printed in the USA
LVOW01s1453210916
505621LV00016B/664/P